Good Versus Evil in the Films of Christopher Lee

AF271321

Good Versus Evil in the Films of Christopher Lee

PAUL LEGGETT

McFarland & Company, Inc., Publishers
Jefferson, North Carolina

ALSO BY PAUL LEGGETT

Terence Fisher: Horror, Myth and Religion (McFarland, 2002)

Frontispiece: **Sir Christopher Lee, circa 1960 (courtesy Ronald V. Borst/Hollywood Movie Posters)**

LIBRARY OF CONGRESS CATALOGUING-IN-PUBLICATION DATA

Names: Leggett, Paul, 1946– author.
Title: Good versus evil in the films of Christopher Lee / Paul Leggett.
Description: Jefferson, North Carolina : McFarland & Company, Inc., Publishers, 2018. | Includes filmography. | Includes bibliographical references and index.
Identifiers: LCCN 2018010736 | ISBN 9781476669632 (softcover : acid free paper) ∞
Subjects: LCSH: Lee, Christopher, 1922–2015—Criticism and interpretation. | Good and evil in motion pictures.
Classification: LCC PN2598.L38 L44 2018 | DDC 791.4302/8092—dc23
LC record available at https://lccn.loc.gov/2018010736

BRITISH LIBRARY CATALOGUING DATA ARE AVAILABLE

ISBN (print) 978-1-4766-6963-2
ISBN (ebook) 978-1-4766-3158-5

Front cover image of Christopher Lee (as Lord Summerisle) in *The Wicker Man*, 1973 (National General Pictures /Photofest)

Printed in the United States of America

McFarland & Company, Inc., Publishers
 Box 611, Jefferson, North Carolina 28640
 www.mcfarlandpub.com

To my grandchildren,
Silas, Hazel, Eli and Faye

Table of Contents

Acknowledgments

I was 13 when I saw my first Christopher Lee film. It was *The Hound of the Baskervilles* (1959) and it remains my favorite Hammer film. When Lee's earlier Hammer films *The Curse of Frankenstein* (1957) and *Horror of Dracula* (1958) were released, I was deemed to be too young for such "horror films." However being a staunch Sherlock Holmes fan and now, 1959, officially a "teenager," I could not be denied. My initial reaction to the film was positive. However upon later reflection I was not so sure about it. Hammer's version was unlike any Holmes film (or horror film, for that matter) I had ever seen. In those days, I feasted on *Shock Theater* with the Universal classics along with the Basil Rathbone Sherlock Holmes films. Hammer was something different. It was not until I saw the film again on television that I realized how good it was.

Over the following years, I followed Hammer's team of Peter Cushing and Christopher Lee in whatever film they appeared. These included non–Hammer films which were never as good as the Hammer product (a film like *Dr. Terror's House of Horrors* comes to mind). But any film with Cushing or Lee, I would eagerly seek out.

In a previous book for McFarland, *Terence Fisher,* I acknowledged many of the friends and supporters who had encouraged me to write about Hammer along with "horror, myth and religion." I especially want to mention the Rev. Tim Gregson who years ago first told me about the exciting world of Hammer Films.

Christopher Lee's death in 2015 was truly the end of an era. It had been a joy to see Lee expand on his already extensive film career by having supporting but nonetheless important roles in *Lord of the Rings* and *Star Wars* movies. The day Lee died, I wore a Christopher Lee t-shirt and I was impressed by the many comments of people of all ages who in effect said, "May he rest in peace."

I greatly appreciate the support and encouragement of the staff and congregation of Grace Presbyterian Church for giving me the study opportunities to work on this project. I also wish to thank the faculty and students at Montclair State University where I teach Mythology part-time for their interest and helpful feedback.

I especially want to thank also Ronald V. Borst of Hollywood Movie Posters for his help in supplying me with photographs for this present book just as he did for my previous book on Terence Fisher.

Thanks to my parents Jane and Joe Leggett, who indulged my interest in fantasy, mystery and horror, and to my younger sister Pam, who endured all this as we were growing up.

I am especially grateful to my wife Beth, who guides and helps me in everything; my daughters Elisabeth and Gwendolyn, and their husbands, respectively Brad and Justin, and my son James, all of whom have provided me with insights and many helpful suggestions.

I want to add a special note on my grandchildren Silas, Hazel, Eli and Faye. They fill my life with joy and happiness.

Finally I must mention Christopher Lee himself. His unforgettable performances in films like *The Devil Rides Out* and *The Wicker Man* have strengthened my own personal faith in Jesus Christ.

In all things, to God be the glory.

Introduction

Christopher Lee is one of the most impressive figures ever to appear on screen. Standing 6'4" with a baritone voice, deep penetrating eyes and an overall commanding presence, he was unforgettable whether on screen or on recordings, (not least of which were his heavy metal versions of Christmas carols). He appeared in over 200 theatrical films, many television episodes and video games. He became famous appearing in the Hammer horror films of the 1950s and '60s. He played Dracula for Hammer a total of seven times. He was the leading screen villain of the second half of the twentieth century.

That only scratches the surface. He was the Marquis St. Evremonde in *A Tale of Two Cities,* Rochefort in *The Three Musketeers,* James Bond's adversary Francisco Scaramanga in *The Man with the Golden Gun*, Saruman in the *Lord of the Rings* movies and Count Dooku in *Star Wars* movies. He was Artemidorus of Cnidos in Shakespeare's *Julius Caesar.* He played Sherlock Holmes three times, Sherlock's brother Mycroft once and Dr. Fu Manchu five times. He was the Duc de Richleau, fighting the forces of evil in *The Devil Rides Out*, and, in perhaps his greatest performance, the pagan cult leader Lord Summerisle in *The Wicker Man.* He was a pirate on at least two occasions and played a number of historical figures, from Rasputin to Prince Philip to Mohammed Ali Jinnah, the founder of modern Pakistan, a role which Lee considered his most significant.

He made appearances in such diverse films as *Airport '77, Return from Witch Mountain, 1941, Charlie and the Chocolate Factory, Boogie Woogie* and *The Corpse Bride.* He was the only member of the cast and crew of *The Lord of the Rings* who actually met J.R.R. Tolkien. In a National Public Radio interview, he gave a detailed account of the Oxford group Tolkien belonged to, "The Inklings," which included C.S. Lewis (*The Chronicles of Narnia*). It was fitting that, Lee having played Prince Philip in a television movie, it was Prince Philip who knighted him in 2009. Sir Christopher Lee passed away in 2015.

How does one do justice to such an influential and impressive career?

It's hard not to be intimidated, even overwhelmed, by Lee both as a subject and a person. *Lord of the Rings* director Peter Jackson writes in his introduction to Lee's autobiography *Lord of Misrule* that he (Jackson), and the entire film crew, saw Lee as an icon. Jackson adds, "I can connect many moments of my life with Christopher Lee's screen appearances." So can we all. But where do we begin? It would take many volumes to do full justice to Lee's acting career, which began with his carrying a spear in the 1948 film version of *Hamlet* and continued up to his narrating *The Time War* (2017).

There are many themes in Lee's broad and lengthy career. One that demands attention, especially for an actor who often portrayed, in George Lucas' terms, the "dark side," is the whole issue of the conflict between good and evil. This central antithesis informs literature, drama, philosophy, politics and religion. We can all relate to this conflict. We have a fundamental sense of goodness and an awareness of the counter-reality of evil. Allowing for the broad range of Lee's career, it still must be noted that he made more so-called horror films than any other genre. Often dismissed as crude exercises in the morbid and the grotesque, horror films deal fundamentally with this conflict, often in spiritual terms. God represents the good while the Devil or Satan is the personification of evil. But this basic distinction is not always clear. Satan, we are told in the Bible, can disguise himself as an angel of light (II Corinthians 11:14). God's judgments on idolatry can seem unjust to us as when God destroys the worshippers of the golden calf (Exodus 32:25–27). Yet the Hebrew, Christian and Islamic scriptures all maintain that God is merciful and just. He represents essential goodness. Humans, however, are free to reject that goodness and plunge themselves and the world into sin, which is essentially just another name for evil.

Philosophers, novelists and poets have struggled with this theme. The classic horror stories *Frankenstein, Dracula* and *Dr. Jekyll and Mr. Hyde* deal with this theme and the conflicting attitudes that arise from it. Frankenstein hopes to make the perfect human being but ends up with a vengeful monster. Dracula appears charming and inviting but he is also seductive and evil. The good and compassionate appearing Dr. Jekyll contains the evil Mr. Hyde within him.

This essential conflict between good and evil constantly confronts us. We face a number of probing questions. First, can we recognize evil? It may be hard to perceive it, especially in daily life with all its confusion and ambiguity. Second, once we are convinced we have perceived it, how do we deal with it? We certainly want to be on the side of good opposing and unmasking evil. Yet what if we are wrong? Neo-Nazis and Ku Klux Klan members convince themselves that they are agents of "good" opposing the forces of "evil." The conflict is not so easy to recognize.

Seen in the context of this ongoing struggle, the films of Christopher Lee are more than entertainment. They are in effect mythical statements of the ongoing battle between good and evil. Often this struggle is played out in Christian terms with Lee usually being the Satanic figure as in his many film performances of Dracula, continuing up to Lord Summerisle in *The Wicker Man* and finally to Saruman and Count Dooku. He could also be the Christian warrior, as in *The Devil Rides Out*.

Lee identified himself as an Anglo-Catholic, essentially a high liturgical form of the Church of England. For a period, he attended and was a participant at St. Stephen's Church, Gloucester Road, where one of the parishioners was T.S. Eliot. The priest at St. Stephen's helped Lee see the similarities between the church and the theater.

This study proposes to examine 16 representative Lee films which deal in different ways with the conflict between good and evil. Lee's personifications of evil took many forms. He could portray the ruthless and ambitions

Christopher Lee (left) relaxes with two other horror film icons, Barbara Steele and Boris Karloff, on the set of *Curse of the Crimson Altar* (1968).

Rasputin or the Chinese leader of a terrorist sect in *Terror of the Tongs* or a paid assassin in *The Man with the Golden Gun*. He brings something distinctive to each of these portrayals. In turn, the viewer is able to experience another dimension of the ongoing struggle between good and evil.

Briefly, here are the films we will be considering and why they were chosen. The first which is essential to any consideration of Lee, or to Hammer in general, is *The Curse of Frankenstein* with Lee as Frankenstein's creation. Lee's signature role as Count Dracula will be referenced in three films, *Dracula* (aka *Horror of Dracula*), *Dracula, Prince of Darkness* and *Satanic Rites of Dracula*. Hammer's *The Mummy* also needs to be included because, among other things, Lee's performance in the title role has not been fully appreciated.

Other Hammer films examined are the historically inspired (but largely fictional) *Rasputin the Mad Monk, The Terror of the Tongs* (the first Hammer film in which Lee received top billing), *The Hound of the Baskervilles, The Devil Rides Out* and *To the Devil a Daughter*. *The Hound of the Baskervilles* is in a chapter on Lee's various Holmes films, three of which have him portraying the Great Detective. Holmes says in the novel *The Hound of the Baskervilles* that in a small way he was combatting evil. Finally Hammer's psychological thriller, *Taste of Fear* (*Scream of Fear*) is included. Lee considered this the best film he made for Hammer.

To explore fully the theme of good vs. evil in Lee's films, we need to look outside his work for Hammer. Some consider *The Wicker Man* the film in which he gave his best performance. There is also the science fiction thriller *Horror Express*. Lee's cold-blooded assassin Scaramanga faces off against "good guy" James Bond in *The Man with the Golden Gun*.

In 1970, Lee and his frequent co-star Peter Cushing worked for Hammer's chief competitor, Amicus. The film *I Monster* was yet another adaptation of Robert Louis Stevenson's *Dr. Jekyll and Mr. Hyde*. This was clear even though the names of the two central characters were changed. Lee is the Jekyll-Hyde central character. This story certainly has good vs. evil at the heart of it. Lee appeared in film versions of the four main British horror classics, *Frankenstein, Dracula, Dr. Jekyll and Mr. Hyde* and *The Hound of the Baskervilles*.

We then need to look at Lee's performances in installments of two epic film franchises, *The Lord of the Rings* and *Star Wars*. Lee plays Saruman the White Wizard in all three *Lord of the Rings* films if one includes the expanded video version of *The Return of the King*. He also appears in this role in the spin-off films based on *The Hobbit*. Lee is Count Dooku in *Star Wars: Episode II—Attack of the Clones* and appears briefly in *Star Wars: Episode III—Revenge of the Sith*. The *Rings* and *Star Wars* films have a spiritual, quasi-mystical aspect to them focusing on the battle between good and evil.

Lee certainly saw the importance and significance of the films in which he appeared. In his commentary on *The Devil Rides Out*, he refers to an exchange that his character, the Duc de Richleau, has with a spirit. Seeking to be certain that the spirit is a good one and not a demon in disguise, de Richleau asks, "Do you acknowledge our Lord Jesus Christ?" The spirit answers, "I do." Lee then adds that this is proof that the spirit is on the side of good and can be trusted.

Christopher Lee himself is clearly on the side of good.

1

The Curse
of Frankenstein (1957)

The Context of the Film

Christopher Lee first came to the attention of international film audiences in Hammer Films' inaugural Gothic horror film *The Curse of Frankenstein* (1957). This was hardly Lee's first film. Before Hammer, he had appeared in a variety of films, all minor roles. He carried a spear in Laurence Olivier's award-winning version of *Hamlet* (1948), a film which also featured his future Hammer colleague Peter Cushing. He also had small roles in *Captain Horatio Hornblower* (1951) and *Moulin Rouge* (1952). None of these portended any kind of stardom. That all began with *Frankenstein* and lasted until his death in 2015.

The success of Hammer with its release of *Curse of Frankenstein* has become a familiar tale in film history. While scorned by critics at the time, the film was an enormous hit, making stars of its leads, Peter Cushing as Victor Frankenstein and Christopher Lee as "The Creature" (a term used more frequently in the film than the familiar "Monster"). It not only established Hammer as the creators of a whole new style of horror film but opened the doors for other small British companies like Amicus and Tygon to market successful horror pictures. *Curse of Frankenstein* also established its director Terence Fisher as the leading figure in British horror for the next decade.

While the film is certainly seen now as a classic and has been the subject of much analysis, the complete scope of Lee's performance as Frankenstein's creation has still not been fully appreciated. Initially Lee's role as the Creature was dismissed as simply being a killing machine without thought or motivation. His appearance, totally unlike that of Boris Karloff in his 1930s Frankenstein films, was actually quite close to Mary Shelley's description of the Monster in the original novel. Most 1950s film critics had little or no awareness of the original novel and dismissed Phil Leakey's outstanding makeup

Christopher Lee as the Creature in *The Curse of Frankenstein* (1957).

as looking like the survivor of a car wreck or, even worse, Jerry Lewis with acne!

Lee's performance as the Creature should not be too readily dismissed. In this writer's opinion, Lee essentially plays the Creature as an abused child. To appreciate this, we have to look at the creation of the Creature in the film.

To begin, Peter Cushing plays Victor Frankenstein as a totally unsympathetic character. He is an obsessed narcissist. He has made his view of science into a god and he believes that he (rather than God) can create the perfect human being. Along the way, he lies, cheats on his fiancée and commits murder.

The Film

Victor Frankenstein, fixated on creating the perfect human being, obtains an athletic body. He manages to get the hands of a sculptor. Finally he adds the brain of a genius by murdering his old physics professor and, after his interment, cutting the brain out of his skull. His effort is thwarted by his former teacher and now assistant, Paul Krempe. The two men have an altercation in the crypt where the professor's body has been laid with the result that the brain is damaged. Undeterred, Frankenstein continues with his creation. Paul remains as a guest in the house but wants nothing more to do with Frankenstein's experiment. The implication is clear that Paul remains because he is concerned about Frankenstein's fiancée who has come to live there and, at the same time, he is clearly attracted to her.

Frankenstein reaches the point where he is prepared to bring his creation to life, but he is unable to work the laboratory apparatus by himself. He goes to Paul's room and persuades him to assist him, promising he will destroy the Creature once he has fully analyzed it. While Frankenstein is out of the lab, we see the most unusual creation scene in any Frankenstein film. In earlier films, Frankenstein deliberately harnessed the power of lightning to bring the Monster to life. In this case, however, lightning suddenly strikes the laboratory and brings the Creature to life without any direct human activity. Frankenstein returns to find the Creature standing erect. Fisher tracks in on the bandaged face of the "perfect being," who rips off the bandage and reveals a hideously scarred face. The Creature then attacks Frankenstein and almost kills him. Paul's arrival on the scene is all that prevents this from happening.

This is a pivotal scene on multiple scores. Of course the creation of the monster is a key moment in any Frankenstein film. Yet here the actual birth of the Creature takes place without Frankenstein himself. It is important to note that in the early Hammer films, especially those directed by Terence Fisher, there are strong spiritual, moral and even religious overtones. An underlying theme of the Frankenstein story going all the way back to Mary Shelley's original novel is the idea that a human being cannot try to take the place of God. What Frankenstein is doing is nothing less than a violation of God's creation. The subtitle of the original novel is "The Modern Prometheus." Prometheus in Greek mythology defied Zeus by bringing fire as a gift to men on Earth. For this, he was severely punished.

A harbinger of the Frankenstein theme can be found in an earlier Hammer science fiction film, also directed by Terence Fisher: *Four Sided Triangle* (1953), on which Fisher also has a writing credit, opens with a verse from the Bible, Ecclesiastes 7:29, "God hath made man upright; but they have sought out many inventions," or in a modern translation, "God made human beings straightforward but they have devised many schemes." Frankenstein is a schemer in the most negative sense. Like Prometheus, he is defying God. In this view, Frankenstein is almost courting divine intervention against his blasphemous project.

The lightning that brings the Creature to life metaphorically can be seen as Zeus' thunderbolt thrown in judgment or, in Fisher's more orthodox Christian view, the lightning which symbolizes God's wrath (Psalm 144:5–6).

The judgment which Frankenstein faces comes in the form of an attack by his creation. But why does the Creature, newly created, immediately attack him? This is where some critics have dismissed Lee's performance as that of a mindless killing machine. Others have surmised that since the Creature has the brain of Frankenstein's murdered professor, he recognizes Frankenstein as his killer and seeks revenge. However, neither of these views can hold up to scrutiny in the light of Lee's overall performance. We are not given any clear clues initially for the Creature's attack. As the film develops, a pattern begins to emerge as to the Creature's motivations and actions.

The thesis that we need to consider is that the Creature finally is an abused child. As an abused child, he lashes out in fear and mistrust. There could be no more abusive parent than Frankenstein. To test this interpretation, we have to look at the full scope of Lee's performance.

After the creature's initial attack on Frankenstein, he is strapped to a laboratory table while Frankenstein plans to study him. However the Creature escapes and wanders off into the nearby forest. It is here that he encounters two figures partly derived from characters in Mary Shelley's novel. The first is a blind man who in the book helps to tutor the Creature. The second is a young boy who resembles the child, William, Frankenstein's younger brother in the book, who is unintentionally murdered by the Monster. In the film we are given a blind man who is out walking with his young grandson. The blind man sits down to rest while the boy runs off. It is at this point that the Creature appears. The blind man hears the sound of the approaching stranger. Frightened, he pokes the Creature with his cane. The Creature initially staggers back. However, responding in anger, he breaks the cane and then kills the old man. We see the little boy returning but we are not shown anything. The presumption is that he is killed too.

Lee captures the idea that the Creature appears frightened. He has no identity initially. The suggestion that the Creature, having the brain of Frankenstein's old teacher, is somehow acting out of revenge cannot be sustained. Not only has the brain been damaged but it has also gone through an electrical birth, as it were. In any event, Lee never suggests a continuity with the aged professor in his performance. He plays the Creature in this scene as a frightened child. There is also the suggestion that the Creature may be in some degree of pain. This becomes much more evident after he is shot. Lee has said that he tried to portray the Creature as being loose-limbed. His arms and legs are not completely responsive to his mind.

These early scenes strongly suggest that the Creature is afraid and lashes out at those around him. After he has been brought to life a second time by Frankenstein, now showing the obvious sign of a head wound, this is even more the case. Frankenstein's spurned mistress, the servant girl Justine (also a character from the original novel which screenwriter Jimmy Sangster claims not to have read but which he clearly had) enters the lab at night trying to find some evidence of Frankenstein's crimes. Frankenstein has set a trap for her: He locks her in the lab with the Creature. When she sees the Creature, she screams and we must conclude that the Creature has killed her. (In spite of the protests at the time of the film's release, much of its violence takes place off screen.)

Fisher sets up the death of Justine in a familiar way. As she looks about the lab, we see what she doesn't see, the shadow of the Creature. In her white nightgown and the Creature's dark clothing, we have an image that goes all the way back to *The Cabinet of Dr. Caligari,*(1920), one that has reappeared in countless films. What breaks the pattern in this scene is the close-up of the Creature. The expression is one of sadness and indeed pain. This is no malevolent monster. Instead it is a forlorn and pathetic figure that emerges. We can presume that the Creature kills the girl primarily to stop her screaming just as the Monster in the original novel unintentionally kills Frankenstein's younger brother in an attempt to stop him from screaming.

The nature of the Creature is underlined definitively at the close of the film. Frankenstein, flushed with what he regards as success in his own mind, brings Paul into his lab to see the Creature. The minute the Creature sees Paul, he turns his face away. Clearly he recognizes the one who shot him earlier. The chained Creature responds to Frankenstein's instructions to stand, walk and sit as though he were some kind of pet.

Outraged by what he has seen, Paul runs to tell the authorities. Frankenstein pursues him. In the meantime the Creature breaks his chain and begins wandering about the lab. Going outside on the roof, he is spotted by Frankenstein and Paul. Frankenstein runs back to the house and grabs a pistol. Elizabeth, Frankenstein's fiancée, hears the commotion and goes into the lab to see what is going on. This is believable because she has no awareness of either the Creature or Frankenstein's crimes. The Creature sees her but when a panel falling from the roof into the lab makes a sudden sound, the Creature retreats. Elizabeth represents no threat to him. When the Creature later encounters Elizabeth on the roof, Frankenstein shoots at him but ends up wounding Elizabeth. We see the rage in the Creature's face as he goes after Frankenstein, recognizing the source of his pain. Frankenstein throws a lantern at him which sets him on fire and the Creature falls into a vat of acid in the lab. This ends the sorry life of the Creature.

In the framing story of the film, Frankenstein in prison has been telling all this to a priest. Paul comes to see him one last time. He denies any knowledge of the Creature and attributes all the murders to Frankenstein. While not technically true, this is morally right since Frankenstein finally is responsible for them. The film ends with Paul and Elizabeth now together (she was only wounded in the arm) and Frankenstein being led out to the guillotine.

Christopher Lee as the Creature

This was the only occasion where Lee played Frankenstein's creation. The overall context of his performance shows the Creature as essentially an abused child. He is primarily abused by Frankenstein who is, in effect, his parent. Lee portrays the Creature as hesitant, fearful, sad and lonely. He is more than capable of violence and he lashes out, more in fear than anything else. However, the Creature is also angry. We see this in the expression on his face when he kills the blind man. His anger is clearly directed at Franken-stein at the end. This is the third critical element which Lee brings to his per-formance. Not only is the Creature frightened and sad, he is angry. These characteristics all fit the profile of an abused child. Tragically, abused children often grow up to become abusers themselves. This is the pattern of the Crea-ture who, from the moment of his creation, is surrounded by people and set-tings which confuse and frighten him.

Lee in his silent characterization is able to communicate all of these fea-tures, making this portrayal one of his best.

Frankenstein's Monster has been portrayed multiple times throughout film history, most notably by Boris Karloff. Karloff too plays the Monster as essentially child-like. In the original 1931 Universal film directed by James Whale, the Monster has, unintentionally, been given the brain of a criminal. In actuality, this is an unnecessary point in the screenplay since all of the Monster's violence arises from specific circumstances. Karloff's portrayal is certainly very effective. He presents the Monster as a child. Frankenstein in this case is hardly abusive. As played by Colin Clive, he is overly tense and seemingly confused by the result of his "experiment." The Monster only becomes violent when abused by Frankenstein's hunchbacked assistant Fritz. Fritz sadistically torments the Monster with whips and fire until the Monster, not surprisingly, kills him. The Monster's next victim is Frankenstein's teacher

Dr. Waldman, who attempts to dissect him. Up to this point, the Monster only appears to be acting in self-defense. Karloff plays him like a frightened child.

There are two subsequent scenes that are clearly echoed in the Hammer version. The first involves the Monster with a little girl. This, as noted, has roots in the original novel. Part of the scene with the little girl in the Karloff version was cut by the censors at the time of the film's reissue in the late 1930s. For many years it was unavailable. In the edited version, the Monster appears to be happily playing with the little girl. Together they throw flowers into a lake. At one point the Monster no longer has any flowers and appears to be reaching out to the little girl. In this version, the scene ends there and in the next we see the girl lying dead in her father's arms. The father says that she has been murdered. In the absence of the full sequence, this suggests a gruesome fate. However, once the sequence was restored, it becomes clear that the Monster in his childlike way throws the girl into the water to see her float like the flowers. When the girl begins to drown, the Monster is obviously very confused and agitated. This scene is portrayed very differently in the Lee version. Here the child is a little boy (as in the original novel). We actually don't see any interaction between the boy and the Creature. But we have just seen the Creature kill the grandfather because he feels he is being attacked. That same anger would then extend to the boy. Lee's actions are consistent with that of an abused child while Karloff's is just that of an innocent who doesn't understand the implications of what he does. In many ways, Karloff portrays the Monster as a newborn. In his first appearance, he reaches out for the sunlight the way a baby might.

The second parallel scene involves the Monster's encounter with Elizabeth, Frankenstein's fiancée. In the Karloff version, the Monster enters Elizabeth's room through a window. He is all in black, Elizabeth is in white as in the archetypical image in *The Cabinet of Dr. Caligari.* However, as a child, the Monster means Elizabeth no harm. He only responds negatively when she screams at his appearance. Karloff's Monster leaves Elizabeth uninjured. The point is that she is no threat to him. In the Hammer version, Elizabeth wanders into Frankenstein's laboratory out of curiosity. In this case, the Creature appears to be almost frightened by her, the reverse of the scene in the Karloff version. When the tile from the roof falls to the floor, prompting Elizabeth to look up, the Creature quickly vanishes. He appears to be leery of her as would be the case with an abused child. When the Creature finally encounters her directly, it is in a confrontation with Frankenstein who fires a shot at him and hits Elizabeth instead. The Creature, sensing this danger, goes after Frankenstein only to be engulfed in flames before falling into the acid vat. In the 1931 version, the Monster fights with Frankenstein in a windmill and ends up hurling the scientist off of the top of the windmill. Here the Monster is reacting to being hunted by Frankenstein and the villagers. He is in effect a scared child.

The most notable difference in the two films is in the scene between the Monster and Elizabeth. In the Karloff version, she is afraid of the Monster. In Lee's version, the opposite appears to be the case. The Creature seems afraid of Elizabeth and in effect tries to hide from her. This is consistent with Lee's portrayal of the Creature not simply as a child but as an abused one. This becomes all the more evident in comparing the two film treatments. In Lee's case it appears that the Creature is seeking to avoid Elizabeth. Like the Karloff version and *Caligari* before it, we have the iconography of the monster in black and the female victim in white. While Karloff's interpretation of an uncertain child who only lashes out when attacked has justifiably been praised, Lee's portrayal of an abused child has not received the acclaim it deserves.

Hammer would touch on the sensitive issue of child abuse in other films. In *Dracula*, the little girl Tania (Janina Faye) is threatened by the vampire Lucy (Carol Marsh), who wants to take her to a secluded place where they can "play." Faye also appeared in a more explicit treatment of child molestation, Hammer's *Never Take Sweets from a Stranger* (1960). This would support the conclusion that Lee's interpretation of the Creature as an abused child was no accident.

Over the course of time, many actors have played the role of the monster. After Karloff left the role, he was followed by classic horror film stars Lon Chaney, Jr., and Bela Lugosi. More recently the creature has been portrayed by Robert DeNiro. In the film *Van Helsing*, Tony Award–winning actor Shuler Hensley briefly played the monster fairly close to Mary Shelley's original conception. While these different actors captured various elements of the monster's vulnerability and even sorrow, only Christopher Lee portrayed him as essentially an abused child.

As impressive as *Curse of Frankenstein* was, Lee's next film role would be even more powerful: In Hammer's *Dracula*, he gave his definitive performance of Count Dracula, the Demon Lover.

2

Dracula (Horror of Dracula) (1958) and *Dracula, Prince of Darkness* (1966)

Prelude to Hammer

Dracula is Christopher Lee's signature role, the part for which he will be most remembered in film history. Lee's long and varied career includes many impressive and diverse performances, several of which we will discuss in subsequent chapters. The full range of his characterizations reads like a who's who of cultural icons including, not only the Frankenstein monster and Dracula, but also the Mummy, Sherlock Holmes (as well as Mycroft Holmes and Sir Henry Baskerville), James Bond's adversary in *The Man with the Golden Gun*, Dr. Fu Manchu, the Comte de Rochefort in *The Three Musketeers*, Saruman in *The Lord of the Rings* and Count Dooku in *Star Wars*, among many others. Yet his performance as Count Dracula is the central achievement of his whole career.

Lee played Dracula in seven Hammer films along with a European version directed by legendary Spanish director Jess Franco, a cameo in Jerry Lewis' *One More Time* (1970) and in Edouard Molinaro's *Dracula and Son* (1976). Lee's essential portrayal of the character was defined in his first two Hammer films, both directed by Terence Fisher, *Dracula* (aka *Horror of Dracula*, 1958) and *Dracula, Prince of Darkness* (1966). His subsequent Hammer Draculas were essentially repeat performances with Lee's increasingly limited portrayal being the sole reason for seeing the films as they degenerated over time, much to Lee's frustration. The first two films are genuine classics and allowed Lee in relatively brief performances to establish a powerful and diabolical image. In these two performances, Lee did more with the Dracula character than anyone else has, before or since.

There were two major versions of *Dracula* prior to Lee's first appearance in the role in 1958. The novel written by Bram Stoker appeared in 1897. The first film adaptation was F.W. Murnau's silent *Nosferatu* (1922). This actually was an unauthorized version which changed the name of the vampire to Count Orlock. This however did not disguise the obvious storyline which led to a suit being brought by Stoker's widow. The result was that the film was suppressed for many years. It finally surfaced in the 1960s. The film is a genuine masterpiece with its Expressionist style and dream-like performances. Dracula (or Count Orlock) however looks scarcely human. He resembles more a demon or a goblin out of medieval folklore.

To this day, the most famous film version is Universal's 1931 adaptation *Dracula*. There is no denying Bela Lugosi's identification with the part even acknowledging that he only played it on-screen twice (the second time being the spoof *Abbott and Costello Meet Frankenstein*). One need only look at a character like "The Count" on *Sesame Street* to see the continuing influence of Lugosi's performance in the role. Yet, as memorable as Lugosi is in the part, his portrayal functions essentially on one level, that of the dark and sinister foreign nobleman. Part of this is due to the fact that the film was based more on the Hamilton Deane stage adaptation than on the original novel. One of the most frightening aspects of Dracula's character is his seductive influence over women. This is scarcely touched on in the film. We have only a very brief scene in long shot of Dracula's first female victim, Lucy, as a vampire. The second woman victim, Mina, is shown under Dracula's influence but there are scarcely any scenes of her and Dracula together. Surely more could have been done to play up this important aspect of Dracula's threat. (The Spanish version that was shot simultaneously with the Lugosi version has a greater erotic aspect but even here there are few scenes of Dracula actually interacting with his female victims.) The Lugosi film, directed by Tod Browning, is genuinely atmospheric but very slow-paced. It reveals only too clearly its stage origins. There is no denying the strong impression that Lugosi makes in the role but the overall treatment of both the character and the story are underdeveloped.

Universal did a few minor sequels, oddly without Lugosi. However by the time of Lee's first attempt at the role, the only real film version anyone knew was the Lugosi one. The time was right for a major new approach to both the character and the story. There were several reasons for this. By 1957 when Lee's first *Dracula* went into production, the United States and Western Europe were in a tense Cold War with the Soviet Union. The space race began that year with the Soviets launching the first satellite. This both demonstrated Soviet superiority in space exploration and added to Cold War tensions. Universal's horror film cycle had ended in the 1940s. In the '50s, there was a focus on science fiction. This yielded a collection of non-human monsters including giant ants, spiders, praying mantises, a Black Lagoon Creature, menacing vegetables, fire-breathing giant lizards (Godzilla) and aliens from outer space. Even when these had a human form, whether in a serious example like *The Day the Earth Stood Still* or a silly one like *Cat Women of the Moon* (or the totally ludicrous but hilarious *Plan 9 from Outer Space*), the threat was external. The central focus of these films was the fear of the other, those who were outside us. The Communist scare, in the hands of figures like Senator Joe McCarthy, led to a clamp-down on everything from films and theater to comic books for fear of "Communist influence." The ultimate statement of this fear in science fiction terms was 1956's *Invasion of the Body Snatchers* where pods from outer space take over Earthlings. The pods assumed the shapes of specific human beings but their souls had been drained out of them. This was an easy metaphor for what was feared to be Communist brainwashing.

The horror film also dealt with a fear of "the other" but not in the sense of radioactive monsters or space aliens. The fear that the horror film portrayed came from within humanity itself. The vampire was a prime example. Vampires were once real people just like us. They were now distorted humans, neither living nor dead but rather the *undead*. The danger was that the vampire or the werewolf or a Dr. Jekyll could be alongside us and appear perfectly normal until the evil within them lashed out. The pod people might look human but one could soon tell by the absence of any kind of emotion that they weren't human. Relatives could easily say, "That's not my mother," daughter, uncle or whatever. On the other hand, the truly frightening thing about the classic monsters is that most of them had been at one time just like us and, to this day, they could appear perfectly normal, barring the rising sun, the full moon or the completion of a forbidden experiment. By 1957 audiences were ready for a revival of the traditional horror film. Hammer demonstrated this with the success of *The Curse of Frankenstein*.

Hammer's obvious follow-up would be *Dracula*. As good as Peter Cushing and Christopher Lee had been in *Curse of Frankenstein*, they would be even better in *Dracula*. Lee read the Bram Stoker novel carefully and was able in a relatively short amount of screen time to convey multiple dimensions of human deceit, desire, cruelty and seduction, drawing on a host of cultural examples from Greek mythology to the Bible to eighteenth and nineteenth century literature.

Before we look at specific facets of Lee's memorable performance, we need to consider another major cultural influence that would play a major role both in the film and in Lee's interpretation of the character. That influence was the beginnings of the sexual revolution.

There had always been an erotic element to the horror film. In the very first so-called horror film, *The Cabinet of Dr. Caligari* (1920), we have the "monster," Cesare the sleepwalker, dressed all in black, attacking a woman in her bed. The woman wears a white nightgown. The undercurrents of lust and sexual assault are present here. There's a near-identical sequence in the first *Frankenstein* (1931) with Boris Karloff's Monster, all in black, threatening Mae Clarke in a white wedding dress. Even the 1936 Universal sci-fi fantasy serial *Flash Gordon* has beautiful women wearing long flowing gowns with bare midriffs. While there is certainly an erotic element to these films, it is very much muted. Far more is suggested than shown.

Yet the original Gothic novels that gave birth to the classic horror film had even clearer undertones of sexuality. In the original novel, the Frankenstein Monster ominously vows to be with Victor Frankenstein on his wedding night. In Bram Stoker's *Dracula,* the female vampires and female victims both strongly suggest sexual desire and sexual domination. Robert Louis Stevenson in his *Strange Case of Dr. Jekyll and Mr. Hyde* gives no specifics but offers this extremely evocative statement about Mr. Hyde: "[H]is every act and thought centered on self; drinking pleasure with bestial avidity from any degree of torture to another." Stevenson's line combining pleasure with torture suggests sado-masochism. The film versions gave Hyde a mistress whom he tortures and eventually kills. In the Sherlock Holmes classic *The Hound of the Baskervilles*, the curse of the hound begins with a nobleman attempting to kidnap and potentially rape a young woman. The central female character of the novel is described in somewhat erotic terms as "being a beauty … of a most uncommon type … she was darker than any brunette whom I have ever seen in England—slim, elegant and tall." She is later described as being "one of the beauties of Costa Rica." While nothing explicitly sexual is said about her, the connotation of a dark, exotic foreign beauty is clear enough.

Nonetheless, even given this heritage and the multiple (perhaps even unconscious) film references, the sexual element in the horror film remained little more than a suggestion. All that changed in the 1950s. While the overt aspects of the sexual revolution emerged in the 1960s, the seeds had all been planted earlier. On the surface, the 1950s appeared to be very circumspect about sexuality. Nudity was unheard of in mainstream movies. In both film and television, married couples were shown having twin beds. Sexual themes were largely absent from mass media storylines. The sexual elements of Hammer's *Dracula* were considered shocking for the period. A scene in the film where Dracula is kissing the heroine Mina *and* drinking her blood was censured in both England and America. That scene will be discussed in detail later. Suffice to say for the moment that the scene was only recently restored to video in England from a copy found in Japan.

The 1950s showed a growing tolerance for sexual themes that had not been seen earlier. Marilyn Monroe's enormous popularity is a major example. Perhaps her two most iconic images were of her nude calendar (later reprinted in the first issue of *Playboy* magazine) and of her dress being blown up by the rush of the subway under the street in *The Seven Year Itch*. In addition to Marilyn, there were Jayne Mansfield and Jane Russell. In England there was Diana Dors. These actresses were able to be provocative in ways that challenged the censorship codes in both England and the U.S. While nudity was still rare, there was plenty of cleavage. The success of *Playboy* brought nudity more into the general cultural context. Most importantly, there was Alfred Kinsey's studies on sexual behavior. Kinsey argued that both men and women were far more active sexually than was generally thought.

Dracula (Horror of Dracula) *(1958)*

All of these elements came into play in Hammer's original *Dracula*. Quite frankly there had never been a horror film like this before, even including *Curse of Frankenstein*. In Hammer's first two Dracula films, Christopher Lee created a character with more depth and resonance than had ever been seen in any horror film, or *any* film of a mythical nature for that matter.

The first appearance of Dracula is intended to throw the audience off-balance. Jonathan Harker arrives at Castle Dracula, ostensibly to work on the count's library. He enters the castle through the unlocked door. Instead of the cobwebbed dark and shadowy Castle Dracula of the Bela Lugosi version, Harker here enters into a pleasant and inviting dining room with a fire blazing and an elegant meal prepared for him. He finds a note from Dracula which says that he is delayed and will return later in the evening. Harker's one off-putting experience is the appearance of a beautiful young woman in a white Grecian dress. She begs Harker to help her but then rushes off as Harker's attention is attracted by a tall, shadowy figure at the top of a staircase. As the figure descends, director Terence Fisher seems to be preparing us for something startling, if not outright frightening. Yet all we get is a close-up of a charming, attractive man who says simply, "I am Dracula. I welcome you to my house." For the first time in film history, Christopher Lee makes his appearance as Count Dracula.

Lee's opening line could not be more different from the ominous, stilted and heavily accented, "I am Dracula. I bid you welcome" that Bela Lugosi intones, backed by a giant spider web in a crumbling castle. On the contrary, Lee is the perfect host, carrying Harker's luggage up to his room and giving him a key to the library since he will be out during the day. Dracula admires a picture of Harker's fiancée Lucy Holmwood and makes the simple comment, "Charming, charming." At this point, there is nothing ominous about his behavior. In a comparable scene in *Nosferatu*, the count's comment on the fiancee's picture is "What a lovely throat." You don't need to have read the novel to realize that something is wrong here. There is no trace of that in Lee's performance. The first thing we notice about the most evil man in the world is his charm and gentility.

Our second exposure is very different—shockingly so. We learn that Harker has in fact come to destroy Dracula, "to end this man's reign of terror." However we the viewer have seen no reign of terror yet nor anything like it. Harker at one point realizes that he has been locked in his room. Later, however, he finds the door open and begins exploring the castle. The candles are all lit but no one seems to be present. Harker enters the library when he finds the strange woman who had accosted him earlier. Claims to be a prisoner of Dracula, she accuses him of incredible evil. Harker's sympathy is aroused. He, somewhat foolishly for a vampire hunter, allows her to embrace him. In a close-up she reveals her fangs as she bites his neck. Suddenly Dracula appears. He could not be more different from what we had seen initially. His mouth and teeth are blood-stained. His eyes are bloodshot. His face has a ferocious appearance. He grabs hold of the vampire woman. When Harker tries to intervene, Dracula chokes him almost to death. Dracula picks up the woman and proceeds to carry her out of the room. Harker passes out.

This is an incredible sequence. Fisher's direction is superb and James Bernard's pounding music score adds to the effect. Nonetheless it is Lee's acting that makes the scene work so well. He seethes with fury throughout the scene. His carrying off the woman indicates that he is not done with her, giving her previous comment about the "terrible things he does" a sexual connotation. The actress is Valerie Gaunt, who played Frankenstein's maid and mistress in *Curse of Frankenstein*. Her appearance is certainly symbolic (where does she get a Grecian dress in nineteenth century central Europe, not to mention high heels?). Whether this was intentional or not on Hammer's part, she does suggest the original iconic victim in *Cabinet of Dr. Caligari* with her long, dark hair and white gown. In the space of about 15 minutes we have seen two very different depictions of Dracula, as congenial host and demonic attacker.

Lee's third scene shows us yet another facet of the character. A revived Harker is determined to destroy both Dracula and the woman by staking them while it is still day and they are confined to their coffins. He finds the vault where both lie in those coffins. However, it is growing late in the day since he has been unconscious through most of it. Rather than destroying Dracula first, he attends to the woman. (Does he have some attraction to her?) As he drives the stake into her heart, she screams. In a close-up of Dracula in his coffin, his eyes open. While not yet able to rise, he knows the sun is going down. The expression on Lee's face is masterful. He displays an evil smile which connotes two things. First he will soon be able to rise since it is almost dark. Second, he now has Harker in his control since Harker is still focused on the staked vam-

Lee as Dracula in Hammer's *Dracula* (aka *Horror of Dracula*) (1958).

pire woman, whom we now see as an elderly woman. Harker turns to Dracula's coffin. To his horror, he sees that it is empty. He has delayed too long with the vampire woman. He turns and sees a shadow descending the stairs to the crypt. Dracula enters silently. Lee displays no ferocious rage nor even a malevolent smile. His face is grim but largely unemotional. He is now the executioner. Harker has been exposed for who he really is, an enemy of Dracula. He therefore must be eliminated. Harker backs away in fear. Dracula closes the door of the crypt. The scene ends. The result is a foregone conclusion. With the exception of his opening scene, Lee does all this without any dialogue. He conveys rage, self-confidence and controlled anger all with just his facial expressions and body movement.

The next appearance of Dracula is in a very different setting. The scene is a Germanic town within a day's ride from Castle Dracula as opposed to the English setting of the original novel. We learn that Harker's fiancée Lucy is suffering from a chronic anemia. We see her prepare herself for bed. She takes off the cross around her neck and lies on her bed with her arms extended almost in the pose of a sacrificial victim. A close-up reveals two bites on her neck. Clearly she has fallen under Dracula's spell. Dracula will indeed enter her room and bend over her to bite her neck. There is nothing in her manner to indicate fear or apprehension. Whether the earlier vampire woman was being deceitful or not, she at least expressed a fear of Dracula and "the terrible things that he does." There is no suggestion of that at all in Lucy's behavior.

Dracula here takes on the character of a seducer or illicit lover. Lucy has entered into a deadly relationship with him. Dracula's whole pose of waiting outside her door on an autumnal night with the leaves swirling and then entering with her in her bed clearly expecting him, is a classic depiction of the illicit lover. She seems glad to give in to his seduction. Prof. Van Helsing's (Peter Cushing) efforts to save her fail when she objects strongly to the garlic flowers he orders to be placed near her bed to ward off Dracula. She dies and becomes a vampire who will have to be staked to be laid to rest.

Dracula as a seducer is a major part of Lee's interpretation of the role. In the case of his next victim, Mina Holmwood, we see the effects of her seduction rather than the seduction itself. While Van Helsing and her husband Arthur are out trying to locate Dracula, she is tricked into going to a funeral home where Dracula lies hidden in his coffin. We do not see her actual encounter with Dracula. We next see her coming into her house in the early morning, claiming to have gone for a walk. She is holding her fur collar tight around her neck and her whole manner suggests that she is hiding something. We the viewers can clearly see that she has become Dracula's victim. We learn later that she is hiding Dracula's coffin in the basement of their home. Knowing that she has been attacked by Dracula, Van Helsing and Arthur stay up all night watching the outside of the house. The irony is that Dracula is already inside.

Up to this point, Mina's dress and attire have been properly Victorian. She wears high collars and long dresses and her hair is tightly bundled up. During the night when her husband and Van Helsing are standing watch, she opens her bedroom door and steps out in a flowing nightgown with her hair down around her shoulders. She, like Lucy, she anxiously awaits the arrival of her dark lover. She see Dracula at the base of the stairs leading up to her room. He comes up the stairs and into her room. She backs away, not avoiding him but positioning herself on the bed. Lee's expression is intense and almost angry. In the restored version of the scene, he caresses and seemingly kisses her before biting her on the neck. The scene ends.

One of the most impressive elements of Lee's portrayal is how much he is able to convey without dialogue. In the sequel *Dracula, Prince of Darkness* he has no dialogue at all but is able to communicate a great deal not only through his facial expressions but also his body. We need to look at the elements of this aspect of his character, the elegant and angry seducer.

In this scene, Mina is obviously apprehensive but at the same time has to be looking forward to her encounter with Dracula. It would only take one scream to bring Van Helsing and Arthur to her rescue—but she doesn't want to be rescued. More disturbing is what Dracula conveys. His expression is not lustful. As noted, there is energy and an element of anger in his expression. He is more than a seducer here. He is expressing dominance. He is overwhelming Mina and even though the encounter nearly costs her her life, she offers no resistance.

Lee here is drawing on multiple archetypes. Whether he and the Hammer crew at that time were conscious of them, they are still present. Dracula is an abusive but compelling lover. His desire is for power far more than sex. The classic image of this is the Greek god Dionysus. Dionysus is known as the god of wine but actually more than that, he is a god of frenzy, even madness. This madness includes his role of a god who promotes the theater. Dionysus traveled with satyrs and women who had been seduced by his wine. These women, known as Maenads, would participate in orgies, often with the satyrs, and virtually lose their identities.

The most famous version of Dionysus in Greek literature is Euripides' play *The Bacchants*. In it, Dionysus comes with his followers to Thebes. He infects the women of the city and draws them into his celebrations and frenzy. The king of Thebes, Pentheus, is understandably upset and wants to put an end to Dionysus' influence. Locking him up proves fruitless as Dionysus easily escapes. Dionysus takes his revenge by disguising himself and enticing Pentheus to observe the depraved celebrations from a safe distance, hidden in a tree. Pentheus agrees to this, unaware that it is a trap. Pentheus is seen by the Maenads who in their madness think he is a mountain lion. They tear him to pieces. His own mother twists off his head and parades around with it as though it were a trophy.

Dracula as played by Lee is a type of Dionysus. He is a demon lover. The first point to note is that he places a spell on women. Dionysus' spell is a combination of wine and sex and leads women into a madness where they can become a danger to themselves and others. Dracula also creates a spell through drinking the women's blood. They fall into a form of madness by following him without restraint. Like the vampire woman in the castle, or Lucy once she has become a vampire and goes after children, they can become a danger to others. Dionysus can disguise himself as a helpful charmer as he does with Pentheus. Dracula can play the same role as we see in his initial encounter with Jonathan Harker. Harker knows Dracula is a vampire but he still allows himself to be locked in his own room

There are other antecedents to Dracula. A very obvious one is the Marquis De Sade (1740–1814). His highly controversial writings frequently put an emphasis on pleasure and pain, the two often expressed through sexuality.

De Sade's work gives indications of sado-masochism. The essence of Dracula's attacks on women is clearly a combination of sexual pleasure and pain. This is shown in both Lucy and Mina. In the extended scene between Dracula and Mina, she communicates both a foreboding and an attraction. The attraction predominates. Lee's Dracula does not ascend the stairs to her room with an expectant look of pleasure. Quite the contrary, as already noted, he looks stern and somewhat angry. Once Mina is on her bed, he kisses and caresses her face and then bites her neck. Pain and pleasure are fused together in that one act. The whole context is sexual.

One of the many failings of later Dracula adaptations, such as *Bram Stoker's Dracula* (1992), is that the sexual aspect of the vampire myth is made explicit. The fact that in Hammer's version it is more suggested and symbolized makes for a richer and more involved symbol. We are dealing here with sexual abuse and yet the women who were victimized sought it. This is a troubling aspect of many cases of domestic violence. Hammer's film and Lee's performance force us to think about the issue.

Another literary antecedent to *Dracula* would be Heathcliff in Emily Bronte's classic novel *Wuthering Heights* (1847). His love for Cathy is far more than an erotic or emotional relationship: His love, or his version of it, involves inflicting pain on Cathy for her failure to marry him. But Heathcliff is presented as something almost more than human. He is a dark force which merges with the windswept moors and inflicts pain and suffering all around him. He has an almost hypnotic effect on women, not only Cathy whom he claims to love, but Isabella, his wife whom he torments. It is certainly not overstating the case to say that Heathcliff is essentially a kind of vampire, draining the life of those around him. Like De Sade and certainly like Dracula, he chooses to inflict pain on people who are ill-prepared to resist it. In Emily's sister Charlotte Bronte's *Jane Eyre*, Rochester also foreshadows elements of Dracula. He is a reclusive nobleman with a dark secret involving his wife, who is locked away in an upstairs chamber.

The most obvious influence on the character of Dracula is certainly the Devil as found in the Bible and Christian tradition. The root of the name "Dracula" refers to "devil" or "dragon," both titles of Satan, the embodiment of evil in the Bible. The Devil is presented less as a frightening figure than as an attractive one. He disguises himself as an angel of light (II Corinthians 11:14–15). In tempting both Eve and Jesus, he pretends to be helpful. He entices Eve with the promise of secret knowledge along with the forbidden fruit (the Bible never says it's an apple) that was "a delight to the eyes" (Genesis 3:6). Satan offers Jesus the opportunity to end his hunger by suggesting he turn stones into bread (Matthew 4:1–3).

Dracula's cordial welcoming to Harker is definitely a Satanic trait. The Devil is seductive, the same way Dracula is with his female victims. The Devil is also described as "a roaring lion prowling about seeking whom he may devour" (I Peter 5:8). Dracula is also capable of furious attacks, as seen in the library sequence.

The real imagery of the Devil comes at the climax. When Dracula captures Mina and takes her to his castle, he is described by the housemaid as looking like "the Devil himself!" Dracula races to get to his castle before daylight since sunlight would destroy him. Van Helsing and Arthur follow. Once at the castle, Dracula tries to bury Mina alive. He is interrupted by the arrival of Van Helsing and Arthur. Dracula runs into the castle with Van Helsing in hot pursuit. They fight in the large banquet hall. When Dracula gets Van Helsing in a death grip, the professor pretends to lose consciousness and is then able to break away. But he is again stalked by the much more powerful Dracula. At that moment, he sees through a slit in the drawn curtains a ray of sunlight. The sun is coming up. In what is still one of the most exciting climaxes to any horror film, Van Helsing jumps up on the table, runs down

The destruction of Dracula in *Dracula* (aka *Horror of Dracula*) (1958).

the length of it and leaps into the air, grabbing hold of the curtains and pulling them down. The room is flooded with light. Dracula lets out a scream as his foot is caught in the sun's rays and disintegrates. Van Helsing then takes two long candle holders and forms them into a cross which drives Dracula into a patch of sunlight, where he disintegrates into dust.

In this closing sequence, we see Dracula truly as a form of "the Devil himself." Two things lead to his destruction. The first is the cross. Later vampires, including Anne Rice's Lestat, seemed largely immune to the power of the cross. This is not so in the classic horror tradition. The imagery here is

A 1958 U.S. newspaper ad for *Horror of Dracula*.

not focused on the sacrificial aspects of the cross with Jesus dying to bear the consequences of human sin. The focus here is on the cross as a symbol of victory. It is in going through the suffering of the cross that Jesus is able to defeat the powers of death, Hell and certainly the Devil. Lee captures this in an agonized expression as the cross, symbol of the defeat of evil, is forcing him further out into the sun's light. His look is one of desperation and hopelessness. He knows he is trapped. If he came in contact with the cross, it would burn him as it did the two women victims.

What finally destroys Dracula is the light. This is a major motif in the Bible. In Bram Stoker's novel, the sun does not destroy the vampire. However, in daylight the vampire has no power. In *Nosferatu* the Dracula figure is destroyed by the sun and that has been a cinematic tradition ever since. Light in the Bible signifies far more than the sun. On the first day of Creation, God says, "Let there be light," and there was light. The sun, moon and stars are not created until the fourth day. Right from the beginning, the theme of light represents something more than physical illumination.

We see this more clearly in the New Testament Gospel of John. Here Jesus himself is identified with light. He is the light of the world. In a crucial opening statement, we are told that the "light shines in the darkness, and the darkness did not overcome it" (John 1:5). Dracula is not only a symbol of the Devil. He represents the darkness as the power of evil. This power is very real but it has no strength against the light. Lee's mournful facial expression as Dracula is being forced out into the light captures the essence of this theme. Following Dracula's destruction into dust, a gust of wind blows the dust away. What does the wind signify? It could be the Holy Spirit which is often described as blowing like the wind. Or it could be something else, something less holy. The answer to this is found in the sequel, *Dracula, Prince of Darkness.*

Dracula, Prince of Darkness *(1966)*

Following the tremendous success of *Dracula* (*Horror of Dracula* in the United States), a sequel was inevitable. *The Curse of Frankenstein,* which hadn't been as successful, led to a sequel the very next year, *The Revenge of Frankenstein.* While Peter Cushing repeated his role as Baron Frankenstein, Christopher Lee was not in the picture. The original monster had been disintegrated in a vat of acid. Lee apparently was concerned about being typecast either as a monster in general or Dracula in particular. Lee played another monster in *The Mummy* released the following year. In between however he took on some non-horror roles albeit still in horror films. He is an honest doctor in *The Man Who Could Cheat Death*. (However, an Italian poster for that film shows Lee with his ominous Dracula face, testifying to Lee's concern about becoming typecast.) Lee also appeared as Sir Henry Baskerville in *The Hound of the Baskervilles,* this time being the victim of the creature of the title rather than playing a monster.

All this is to say that when Hammer did do a Dracula sequel, it was without Lee. In *The Brides of Dracula,* Peter Cushing reprised his role as Van Helsing but the vampire in the film was presented as a disciple of the dead count. Five more years would pass before Lee would relent and return to the character of Dracula—but this time, Cushing did not reappear as Van Helsing. In *Dracula, Prince of Darkness*, the part of a Christian warrior went to Andrew Keir as a forceful monk named Father Sandor. Terence Fisher returned as the director.

Much has been written about *Prince of Darkness* from a number of angles including a chapter in a book on Terence Fisher by this author. Some have felt the film was a disappointment after the achievement of the first *Dracula*. Others have championed it, including a few who have argued that it was in fact superior to the previous two Hammer Draculas. Perhaps the most controversial part of the film did not involve Christopher Lee. This was a sequence where a group of priests hold down a vampire woman and stake her. While the stakings in previous films involved vampires lying quietly in their coffins (or in one case in *Brides of Dracula* a vampire woman consents to being staked as a way of being purged), in this case Barbara Shelley, in the role of the vampire woman, fully awake and conscious, twists and squirms and even tries to bite her captors. Some felt that this came dangerously close to a symbolic gang rape. As important as that question is to any ultimate evaluation of the film, it lies outside the purview of a study of Lee's role.

The fact that Lee has no dialogue in the film has often been credited to Lee's complaining about the quality of the script. Whatever the final reason, we need to remember that Lee had very limited dialogue in the first film so this was hardly a major departure. In this sequel we learn several things. First of all, Dracula has a human servant, Klove, in his employ. Two English couples are lured to the castle despite Father Sandor's warning to avoid the place. The couples have never heard of Count Dracula but they are informed by Klove that he is dead. Klove serves them an elegant dinner which brings up memories of Harker's fine dinner which turned out to be his last. Klove invites them to spend the night. Mysteriously their luggage appears in their rooms. In the middle of the night, one of the couples, Alan and Helen, are lured successively out of their bedroom. Alan is the first victim. In what was a grisly sequence for the time, he is knocked unconscious and is then chained by his feet upside down over a coffin. His throat is slit by Klove and blood pours down into the coffin. Now we learn what happened to Dracula's ashes: Klove has preserved them. As the blood pours down, Dracula materializes.

Terence Fisher apparently intended this scene to be a form of ritual sacrifice. The equation with the Devil is obvious from even the title of the film. When Alan's wife Helen is lured into the crypt, she screams at the sight of her dead husband. At this point, Dracula appears. Helen has been fearful all along of the castle and of Klove. Now, confronted with Dracula himself, she appears neither frightened nor enticed. She can only look blankly at a dark fate. There is no suggestion of caressing here. Dracula spreads his cape over her and we know she will be bitten although we are not shown that.

Satan imagery is present but there is an additional theme that is even stronger in Lee's portrayal in this film. He portrays Dracula as a type of Antichrist. Dracula here represents a number of inversions of Christian themes. Dracula certainly has been a symbol of the Devil or of evil in general. This is true as far back as Murnau's *Nosferatu*. This film, which actually contains layers of symbolism, brings Dracula more into the specific province of the Antichrist. Whether this was due to the screenplay by Jimmy Sangster and Anthony Hinds (both writing under pseudonyms), Fisher's direction or to Lee's own contribution to the role, the net effect is the same. Whatever weaknesses exist in the film's screenplay or dialogue, this focus on the symbol of the Antichrist in a year when *Time* magazine posed the question "Is God Dead?" is certainly very striking. To appreciate this emphasis, we need to look at the figure of Antichrist at least in his initial appearance in the Christian New Testament.

While the theme of the Antichrist is discussed several times in the New Testament even by Jesus, the name only occurs in the first letter of John, one of the shorter books in the New Testament. John defines the Antichrist largely as a spirit that inverts the meaning of Jesus Christ by insisting that Jesus did not come in human form as the gospels maintained. For John there were many Antichrists. That is to say that this spirit could work on any number of individuals who in effect were falsely claiming to be Christians by twisting the meaning of who Jesus actually was. Other accounts refer to a leader who at the end of history will rise up against God and will finally be defeated by Christ. The danger, however, is that this figure, following John's concern, will distort the truth and deceive many people.

His first appearance in the Bible is actually found in the Hebrew Scriptures or Old Testament, in the Book of Daniel. Daniel describes a real historical figure Antiochus Epiphanes who invaded Jerusalem in the second century B.C.E. and went to the extreme of slaughtering a pig on the altar of the Holy of Holies in the temple. For the Jewish people, this was an unbelievable sacrilege and led to the Maccabean revolt. Daniel's description however is not only of a historical figure but this figure Antiochus Epiphanes symbolizes a figure who will appear at the end of time to carry out even greater sacrilege and usher in a "time of anguish, such as has never occurred since nations first came into existence" (Daniel 12:1). Jesus later will warn of the "desolating sacrifice" spoken of by the prophet Daniel (Matthew 24:15).

It can be seen from these brief comments that the Antichrist is a complex figure. Dracula as a type of Antichrist is not a political figure (although a later Hammer Dracula, *The Satanic Rites of Dracula*, begins to get into that realm). Dracula represents the Antichrist in the sense that he is an inversion, a distortion of Jesus Christ. We see this in Dracula's initial appearance in the film. We have a resurrection that begins with a blood sacrifice without which the resurrection could not occur. There could be no resurrection without the death of Jesus first. More than that, the resurrection of Jesus promises eternal life to his followers. Dracula's resurrection will also bring essentially eternal life, not a life of promise, hope and joy but rather the continuing life of the undead.

The initial appearance of the Antichrist in the form of Antiochus Epiphanes involved sacrilege in the context of a sacred sacrifice, that being the sacrifice that was made once a year in the Holy of Holies to atone for the sins of the people (Yom Kippur, Leviticus chapter 16). Since, as Jesus noted, the hallmark of the Antichrist will be a "desolating sacrifice," in the Christian context that would apply to the sacraments since those are the symbols of Christ's sacrifice on the cross. All branches of Christianity accept two fundamental sacraments, Baptism and the Lord's Supper (Holy Communion or the Mass). Dracula offers a "desolating sacrifice" of the Lord's Supper at the onset of the climax of *Prince of Darkness*.

Having escaped from Dracula's castle, Charles and Diana (the choice of names being an interesting foreshadowing of the famous royal marriage) take refuge in Father Sandor's monastery. Diana has been left in a bedroom to recover from the trauma of the recent events. She hears the voice of her sister-in-law Helen, who now is a vampire. Helen claims to have escaped from Dracula and begs to be let in: "It's so cold." Moved by her anxious request, Diana opens the door. Dracula suddenly emerges, biting her hand. Her scream brings help but it is too late. Dracula and Helen are now both in the monastery. Their presence there alone brings up the image of desecration.

Two critical things occur here which relate both to the Antichrist and to Satan. First, there is the issue of deception. Both Antichrist and Satan are masters of deception, "disguised as angels of light" (II Corinthians 11:14). Diana has been deceived into helping Dracula. The second is a classic theme with Biblical roots, the idea of inviting evil into your home. It cannot cross the threshold without being invited. The origin of this idea goes back to the beginning of the Biblical book of Genesis. In chapter 4, God warns Cain, "Sin is lurking at the door; its desire is for you, but you must master it." This led to the view that sin or evil crouches outside the door of your house (or heart), waiting to be let in. Diana falls into this trap when she allows Helen, and also Dracula, into the monastery.

This leads to a striking scene which is an inversion of the Communion Service or Mass. Dracula lures Diana into an empty room. He proceeds to hypnotize her, making her take off her cross necklace. He then opens his shirt and with his long fingernail cuts his chest. The blood slowly pours out. He proceeds to put his hand behind Diana's head and draws her to the blood. Clearly he wants her to drink it. This is based on a scene taken from the original novel in which Mina drinks the blood from Dracula's arm. In the film, Diana is saved when Father Sandor and Charles enter the room. She passes out and Dracula lifts her up in his arms and prepares to take her back to his castle. In the Communion Service, the believer drinks wine which is the symbol of Jesus' blood shed on the cross for the forgiveness of sins. Diana's drinking the blood of Dracula would be a horrific inversion of the sacred meal.

The second reference to a sacrament comes at the end of the film. In daylight, Dracula and Diana are both in coffins in a carriage that is driven by Klove. Father Sandor and Charles are in pursuit. Charles shoots Klove and the horses bolt, stopping at a ridge by the castle. One coffin slides out and lands on the frozen moat outside the castle. This turns out to be Dracula's coffin. Charles steps out onto the moat carrying a stake with which he plans to destroy Dracula. Before he can do so, the sun goes down and Dracula springs out of his coffin, grabbing Charles and commencing to choke him. Above on the ridge, Diana implores Father Sandor to shoot Dracula with his rifle. The monk answers that it would do no good since bullets could not harm Dracula. In desperation she takes the rifle and shoots. The bullet hits the ice and water begins to spring up. Lee's Dracula looks at the water with a mixture of fear and apprehension. Father Sandor, now remembering that running water can destroy Dracula, continues to fire bullets into the ice until Dracula is left on a small floating cake of ice and then proceeds to sink. Dracula lets out one last shriek as the water closes over him. The running water symbolizes the water of baptism which is often poured over the recipient. Baptism symbolizes death and rebirth following the example of Jesus' death and resurrection. In the water of Baptism, sin (and evil) is washed away,

The film ends with the destruction of Dracula, the Satan-Antichrist figure, through the revival of Christian liturgy rather than the inversion of it which we saw in the earlier scene where Dracula was trying to make Diana drink his blood. The "desolating sacrilege" has been destroyed. Lee's performance in these two films reveal multiple levels of symbolism as we have noted from sources as varied as Greek mythology, English literature, Western history and the Bible. Lee's Dracula performance conjures up these various references to Dionysus, the Marquis De Sade, the Bronte sisters, Satan and the Antichrist. No one, before or since, has presented such an in-depth and rich performance of Dracula as Christopher Lee. With all due respect to Bela Lugosi, Frank Langella, Gary Oldman and others, Lee stands alone as the definitive Dracula.

3

The Mummy (1959)

The Context of the Film

Following the success of *Dracula* (*Horror of Dracula*), Universal was only too happy to allow Hammer access to all their movie monsters. A logical choice was to re-film *The Mummy*. Universal actually had two Mummy characters, the first showcased in a dark, moody 1932 film with Boris Karloff, the other in a 1940s series of films with Tom Tyler (in the first) and Lon Chaney, Jr. (in the others), as a lumbering agent of destruction. The two really have little to do with each other except for the central theme of a mummy brought to life to search for his lost love. Hammer's version with Lee in the title role draws on both, but in many ways it's quite different.

Universal turned to the subject of the Mummy following the success of their initial horror films *Dracula, Frankenstein* and *Murders in the Rue Morgue*. The idea of *The Mummy* stemmed in part from literary works like Bram Stoker's *Jewel of the Seven Stars* and Sir Arthur Conan Doyle's short stories "Lot No. 249" and "The Ring of Thoth." However the greatest impetus for the film was the discovery in 1922 of the tomb of Egypt's King Tut. When the leader of the expedition, Lord Carnarvon, died six months after the discovery, there was widespread speculation about a curse on the tomb. This became a favorite topic of the press. This led to Universal's decision to do a film on the desecration of an Egyptian tomb.

The 1932 version was directed by Karl Freund, who had filmed German classics like *The Golem* and *Metropolis* as well as Universal's *Dracula* and *Murders in the Rue Morgue*. The only time we see a bandaged mummy is in the opening which ranks as one of the most unforgettable sequences in the horror films of this period. With a newly unearthed mummy in its sarcophagus nearby, a young archaeologist begins reading a scroll. Behind him, the Mummy starts coming to life, slowly uncrossing its arms. In shock the young archaeologist goes mad with insane laughter as the Mummy carries the scroll away. This is a truly frightening film moment which still holds up 85 years later.

That is the last we see of the Mummy in bandages. We next encounter him as an mysterious Egyptian who calls himself Ardath Bey (Boris Karloff). We subsequently learn that he is the resurrected high priest Imhotep, now in search of the reincarnation of the Egyptian princess (Zita Johann) he loved 3700 years ago. His attempt to kill her so that she can be subsequently resurrected eternally is thwarted when the desperate woman cries out to the statue of the goddess Isis for protection. The statue extends its arm and sends out a thunderbolt which destroys Imhotep.

Universal returned to this theme eight years later. In *The Mummy's Hand* (1940), the Mummy, still in bandages, stalks his victims in a partially paralyzed manner, dragging one foot. The Mummy is not so much reborn through an ancient incantation as by the boiling of tana leaves, whose juice restores him. He remains in search of his lost Egyptian love, the Princess Ananka. The Mummy in this film of the new series was played by Western star Tom Tyler. In sequels, all basically containing the same plot of the Mummy attacking people as he searches for the princess' latest reincarnation, the part of the Mummy was played by Lon Chaney, Jr., who literally shuffles from film to film. The series continues with *The Mummy's Tomb* (1942), *The Mummy's Ghost* and *The Mummy's Curse* (both 1944). The one striking note in these increasingly formula films is the reincarnation of the princess actually turning into a mummy herself as she is carried off at the conclusion of *The Mummy's Ghost.* Over the course of the series, the Mummy becomes an increasingly pathetic figure. We the viewers seemingly want to shout to the intended victims in the films, "Run!" Given the fact that the Mummy only has one good leg, he could be easily outrun but invariably the victims cooperate by allowing themselves to be backed into a corner where he can strangle them. The final entry in the series, as seemed to be the fate of all Universal monsters, was *Abbott and Costello Meet the Mummy* (1955), filmed two years before Hammer launched its rebirth of the classic horror film cycle.

Hammer's 1959 version of *The Mummy* was their fifth Technicolor Gothic Horror film and their fourth to co-star Peter Cushing and Christopher Lee. Unlike *Curse of Frankenstein, Dracula* and *The Hound of the Baskervilles,* all of which were based on classic novels, *The Mummy* was based on Universal's Mummy movies. The script for the 1932 version had been credited to John L. Balderston, who had also worked on Universal's *Dracula* and *Frankenstein* screenplays. A number of lesser writers—Griffin Jay, Maxwell Shane, Henry Sucher, Bernard Schubert—worked on the 1940s series.

As Hammer prepared to re-film *The Mummy*, they were faced with a series of challenges. The first and most obvious question was which version of *The Mummy* were they going to do? Would they try to re-film the 1932

Karloff version or the 1940s series? In reality, there were two Mummy subjects, Imhotep and Kharis. While both captured the idea of a forbidden love, the desecration of an Egyptian tomb and a revived and vengeful Mummy, the working-out of these two themes was very different. Hammer writer Jimmy Sangster was given the daunting task of trying to combine the best of both Universal's versions of the character. Terence Fisher again directed. Cushing again played the lead character and Lee was again given the task of bringing a monster to life, figuratively and literally. The result, as we will see, was one of Hammer's best efforts and one of Lee's most outstanding early performances.

The Film

Sangster blends together elements from both Universal versions of *The Mummy* with the result that he creates a new approach to the familiar story. The film opens with an archaeological excavation at the tomb of the ancient Egyptian priestess Ananka. The British expedition is warned by Mehemet (George Pastell), a high priest of the god Karnak, that they are committing a sacrilege. The head of the expedition, Dr. Stephen Banning (played by the distinguished Shakespearean actor, Sir Felix Aylmer), dismisses the warning and orders the tomb to be blown open with explosives. Before continuing with the effort to enter the tomb, Dr. Banning is reminded by his assistant Joseph Whemple (Raymond Huntley) that his (Banning's) son John (Cushing), the real leader of the expedition, is laid up with a broken leg. Whemple protests that without proper care, John runs the risk of the broken leg knitting improperly. This is what happens since John shares the same concern as his father to proceed with the expedition while weather conditions are favorable. As a result, John walks with a limp through the remainder of the film.

The first major change Sangster makes from the Universal film is that it is Stephen Banning, rather than a young assistant, who first goes into the tomb once it is open and begins reading the sacred scroll. From outside, John and Whemple hear screams. They hurry into the tomb to find that Banning has gone mad from some shock. Unlike the 1932 original film, we do not see what frightened him out of his mind.

The action shifts to England. The year is 1895. This is a different time and setting than the earlier Universal films. Stephen Banning has been placed in a sanitarium. He regains his senses, summons John and tells him what terrified him that day in the tomb of Ananka. In flashback we see the Mummy (Lee) come to life as the elder Banning reads the scroll. What neither father nor son know is that the Mummy, Kharis, is now in England, brought there by the Egyptian priest who had warned them against opening Ananka's tomb.

The role of as priest guiding the bandaged Mummy was a staple of Universal's 1940s series. Invariably the Mummy was looking for the reincarnation of his lost love, Princess Ananka. The standard storyline had the shuffling Mummy taking vengeance on those who had violated her tomb and also attempting to re-capture his lost princess. In a flashback scene from the original film which was reused twice in the 1940s series, we see Imhotep stealing the sacred scroll of Thoth in order to raise his beloved princess from the dead. In the original Universal film, the female lead Helen Grosvener (Zita Johann) really is the reincarnation of the Egyptian princess, originally known as Ankh-es-en-amon but later shortened to Ananka for the 1940s series. At the climax of the 1932 *Mummy*, Helen acknowledges that she is indeed the reincarnated princess and that the ominous Ardath Bey is in reality her ancient lover Imhotep. Imhotep explains to her that she must die in order to be resurrected to eternal life (not unlike Dracula's victims). As noted above, she is delivered from Imhotep by the statue of the goddess Isis. In the 1940s films, Kharis, the re-named Mummy, is usually prevented from being reunited with Ananka's incarnation by the fact that the priests involved end up having lecherous designs on her. The Mummy kills the lustful priest and continues his unrequited love into the next installment where essentially the same thing happens all over again.

Hammer's *The Mummy* has a different take on all this. First, and most importantly, there is no reincarnation of Ananka in the film. But John Banning's wife Isobel (Yvonne Furneaux) looks like Ananka. She has no memory of ancient Egypt or longing for Kharis. Second, the high priest who brings Kharis to England is bent only on killing the "unbelievers" who desecrated the princess' tomb. There is no reference to searching for the reincarnation of the princess. In fact, in a scene not found in any of the Universal films, John Banning goes to the rented home of Mehemet the Egyptian priest, and intentionally baits him by dismissing Egyptian religions as having no substance. Twice Kharis is prevented from killing John by the intervention of his wife, whom the Mummy thinks is Ananka. When the priest cries out for Kharis to kill her, the Mummy instead kills him. At the end, as he carries her into the swamp, she instructs him to let her down, which he dutifully does. Unlike the swamp scene in *The Mummy's Ghost,* she herself never turns into a mummy. The Mummy then is shot many times and sinks into the swamp holding aloft the scroll which brought him back to life.

The biggest and most significant change Hammer brought to the theme of the mummy is the emphasis on Kharis as a tragic lover. The flashback

Lee as the high priest Kharis in *The Mummy* (1959) with unidentified extras.

scene of the death of Ananka and Kharis (or Imhotep) is more extensive in the Hammer version than in any of the Universal films. While the film is well-directed by the erstwhile Terence Fisher and Sangster's script effectively blends elements of the older films with his own approach to the story, the central focus of the film remains the title character of the Mummy whose suffering love for his lost princess is neither ominous nor threatening as in the earlier films. More than anything else, it is tragic. To appreciate this, we now need to look at Christopher Lee's performance.

Christopher Lee as Kharis

Christopher Lee gives two performances in *The Mummy*. In one, he is an Egyptian priest. In the other, he is the bandaged Mummy. The first is a speaking role. The second is performed in mime as he had done in *The Curse of Frankenstein*. This second role must be regarded as one of Lee's finest performances.

Lee's Egyptian high priest does not give the voiceover narration of what took place in ancient Egypt as in the Universal version. Here the narrator is John Banning, who is giving the background information on the Mummy. In this narration, we learn two critical points. First, the love that Kharis has for the princess is forbidden. This point is not stressed in the earlier Universal films. Second, Kharis is presiding over her funeral arrangements. The beautiful Ananka has died. Lee's Kharis conveys a deep sadness in both his voice and his facial expressions. There is no assurance that Kharis and Ananka ever were lovers. In fact, in the Hammer version we never see the actual Princess Ananka alive (Isobel Banning only looks like Ananka, she is not a reincarnation). We are never told whether Ananka herself has any feelings for Kharis. This is totally different from the 1932 film where even the reincarnated princess acknowledges her love for Imhotep. There is no confirmation in Lee's version that Ananka ever had the same love for Kharis that he had for her. This makes his attempt to bring her back from the dead doubly risky. First, such an action is forbidden. Second, even if he were able to bring her back, would she want to be with him, would she love him at all?

In Lee's portrayal of the revived Mummy, his role of tragic lover is stressed even more. One huge improvement over the earlier films is that Lee's Mummy is a fast-moving, dynamic killer when sent out to kill the "unbelievers." This is not a mummy you can easily run away from. At the same time, the Mummy's body movements are striking. Lee doesn't so much walk as lurch forward with his lengthy strides. The most telling part of Lee's performance is when the Mummy encounters what he sees as an apparition of his long-lost princess. Isobel Banning saves her husband from being strangled by the Mummy by simply crying out, "No!" The Mummy looks at her and is startled by what he sees. Using only his eyes and his body movements, Lee conveys the sense of longing and desire that Kharis has for her. He reaches out to her. When she doesn't respond, he lowers his head and his eyes convey a deep sadness. We are left with the question, is this a re-enactment of the ancient past? Had Kharis earlier reached out to the princess only to be rebuffed by her because such a love was forbidden?

At the climax, there is a similar encounter. Once again the Mummy has been sent out to complete the mission of revenge of the tomb desecrators. Again, Kharis has John Banning in his grip just as his wife enters. She orders the Mummy to release her husband. But this time she has her hair up, the Mummy doesn't recognize her and continues to assault her husband. He cries out for her to let down her hair (a clear reference to the fairy tale "Repunzel"). She does so and then the Mummy recognizes her as Ananka.

At this point, Mehemet tells the Mummy to kill Isobel. This reveals the essential conflict of good vs. evil in this film. The issue is not Egyptian religion vs. Christianity, which does come out in John Banning's earlier meeting with Mehemet. The real issue is Mehemet's bloodthirsty desire for revenge and Kharis' tragic, lost love. Mehemet has no interest in Ananka either in the past or present. He only wants revenge on those who defied the gods of Egypt, which is to say, those who have defied him. Kharis is in effect a slave doing his bidding. Everything changes when the image of Ananka enters the scene. Kharis' desire is not for the gods of Egypt in whose name he has been condemned to an eternity of suffering. His sole desire is for Ananka. Confronted with the issue of whether or not to obey Mehmet's command to kill Isobel, he makes the obvious choice of killing Mehemet instead.

Isobel faints. Kharis takes her up in his arms and carries her out into the swamp. This references the final scene in Universal's *The Mummy's Ghost*. That film likewise concludes with the Mummy carrying the reincarnation of Ananka, who has also fainted, into a swamp—and as he does so, she herself turns into a mummy and the two of them disappear into the swamp. But in

The Mummy (Christopher Lee) attacks John Banning (Peter Cushing) in *The Mummy* (1959).

Hammer's version, Isobel Banning is not really Ananka. At her husband's instruction, she tells the Mummy to let her down as they come into the swamp. Kharis does so but with a forlorn, sad expression, as if to say he has once again lost his true love. Had Ananka ever encouraged him? Had she ever expressed any love for him? We are not shown anything in this film to suggest that. Once the Mummy lets Isobel down, she crosses over to the side of the swamp where she is rescued. The police and the villagers led by Banning now shoot the Mummy.

Lee's portrayal of the Mummy conveys a tragic sadness. He does this without any dialogue, using only his eyes and body movements. What we really have here is an unrequited love that has endured for thousands of years. In reality this may well have been the third time that Kharis has lost Ananka. He would have lost her when she must have rejected his forbidden love initially. He lost her again when she died and he has lost her a third time in the image of Isobel. Lee's Mummy is not a menacing monster which many of us went to the theater expecting. Instead he emerges as a supreme example of the doomed lover. Terence Fisher, who called *Dracula* a love story, would return to this theme again in other films, most notably the 1962 *The Phantom of the Opera.*

A final comment on this film: It features echoes of Alfred Hitchcock's *Vertigo* which had been released the year before. In that film, we have a woman (Kim Novak) who is the image of another woman with whom she is confused. In the Hitchcock film, she puts her hair up to resemble the other woman, the reverse of Isobel Banning letting down her hair. Clearly Hammer was aware of Hitchcock's films as you will see in the chapter on *Taste of Fear.*

4

Taste of Fear
(*Scream of Fear*) (1961)

Christopher Lee said that *Taste of Fear* was the best Hammer film he ever appeared in (Lee, p. 242). This is saying a lot. At the time of its release, it was not what was expected from Hammer. It's hard to call it a horror film since it seems more of a suspense thriller. Yet it has its share of shocks. It is clearly influenced by the Henri Clouzot classic *Les Diaboliques* (1955). It has also been compared to Alfred Hitchcock's *Psycho*; it was already in production when *Psycho* debuted. Because of Lee's high praise and the atypical nature of this early 1960s Hammer film, it must be included in any representative list of the films of Christopher Lee. The film was not a great success in Great Britain or the U.S. but it was a huge hit on the European continent. This led to Hammer doing a series of suspense thrillers over the next ten years.

The Context of the Film

By 1960, Hammer had established themselves internationally as the world's leading producer of Gothic horror films. These films were made in Technicolor with impressive direction, sets, music and invariably a nineteenth century setting. Beginning with *The Curse of Frankenstein* in 1957, Hammer released nine Gothic films in this style over the next three years. Lee appeared in six of them: *The Curse of Frankenstein, Dracula, The Hound of the Baskervilles, The Mummy, The Man Who Could Cheat Death* and *The Two Faces of Dr. Jekyll*).

These films were not the studio's sole product. Before the Frankenstein and Dracula films, Terence Fisher had directed a number of Hammer mystery-thrillers: *The Last Page, Mantrap, Face the Music, Blood Orange. The Snorkel* (1958) was a tight suspense film with a twist at the end. In addition to Gothic horror following the success of *Curse of Frankenstein*, Hammer had released a number of war films (*The Steel Bayonet, The Camp on Blood*

Island, Yesterday's Enemy) and comedies (*Further Up the Creek, I Only Arsked, The Ugly Duckling*—the latter a Jekyll and Hyde spoof). There was also science fiction (*The Abominable Snowman*) and costume adventures (*The Sword of Sherwood Forest*).

Nevertheless, *Taste of Fear* was something new for the company. It drew on multiple sources including Hammer's earlier mysteries and aspects of their horror films as well as the aforementioned *Diaboliques*.

Taste of Fear owed its inception to writer Jimmy Sangster. Sangster had written or co-written most of the Gothic horror films that had given the studio its international reputation (*Curse of Frankenstein, Dracula, The Revenge of Frankenstein, The Mummy, The Man Who Could Cheat Death, The Brides of Dracula*). Apparently he wanted to try something new. The result was a draft entitled *See No Evil*. The final script was titled *Taste of Fear* (*Scream of Fear* in the U.S.). In addition to writing, Sangster also co-produced the film with Michael Carreras. It starred Susan Strasberg, the daughter of famed director Lee Strasberg and his wife Paula (who was on the set during production). The success of this film would lead to a series of Hammer psychological thrillers on the borderline of suspense and horror: *Maniac, Paranoiac* and *Nightmare*).

The Film

Given the nature of this film, it must be said at the outset that any summary of its story includes a number of spoilers. The opening scene shows several men in what we will learn is Switzerland, fishing out of the sea the body of a dead girl. Shortly after, we are introduced to Penny Appleby (Susan Strasberg), a young woman who is confined to a wheelchair following a horseback riding accident. For the ten years after her parents' divorce, she lived with her mother. Her mother has now died and Penny's only close friend, Maggie Freeman, had recently committed suicide by drowning herself. This was presumably the young woman whose body we saw being pulled out of the water in the opening scene.

Arriving in Nice, France, Penny is met by her father's chauffeur Bob (Ronald Lewis). In her discussion with Bob, we learn that she has returned to France at the invitation of her father, whom she has not seen in ten years. Bob alludes to her father being ill but gives no further details. Penny has never met Dad's new wife Jane (Ann Todd), who welcomes her warmly to their large, impressive home. Penny learns that her father was suddenly called away on an urgent business matter. Even though it has been ten years she recognizes his picture. Bob and Jane appear to be the only people living in the house. A housekeeper comes in on a daily basis. The only other person who is referred to is her father's friend Dr. Gerrard (Christopher Lee), who comes for dinner.

That night, Penny is awakened by a banging sound outside her room. She makes her way to a window and sees a light in the summer house across the courtyard from her room. Investigating, she enters the summer house and to her horror she finds her father sitting in a chair in a candlelit room, apparently dead. In her haste to get away, the wheelchair gets too close to a deep courtyard pool and she falls in. Bob gets her out of the pool and Jane calls for Dr. Gerrard.

Everyone tries to explain to her that she could not have seen her father. He is away on a trip. She insists on being taken back to the summer house. There is no trace of the body. Dr. Gerrard prescribes some sleeping pills. He insists that she has had a dream or even some kind of hallucination. Jane agrees with this, which only seems to make Penny more anxious.

Penny also see her dead father in her room. She hears a piano playing only to be told that her father was the only one who played the piano and that the piano is locked. In the midst of all this, she receives a phone call from her father, who promises that he will return as soon as possible.

Dr. Gerrard makes Penny even more anxious by raising the possibility that the cause of her physical disability may be rooted in her mind. The doctor asks if she has been examined lately to see if her legs really are crippled. Penny, indignant, insists that she had a riding accident with the horse falling on her, breaking several bones in her back. Jane attempts to calm Penny down.

Things become more suspicious when Bob the chauffeur confides to Penny that he found candle wax on the summer house floor, which supports Penny's story. He confides more and more in Penny and shares her suspicions that her father may really be dead. Bob raises the question of where the body could be kept, how is it being preserved? Bob suspects that the deep pool is where Penny's father's corpse is being preserved. Jane advises Penny to be careful about getting into a relationship with Bob.

Bob dives into the deep pool and finds the body of Penny's father. After he tells Penny, he maintains that the local police are not up to the task and suggests they drive to a larger, neighboring town. It is night. Bob tells Penny to wait at the entrance of the house while he gets dressed and brings the car around. Bob positions Penny in the back seat and begins to drive.

As they are driving, Penny wonders aloud if her stepmother killed her father. Bob suggests the motive may simply may be greed. He intimates that Jane may have had an accomplice. Penny suggests that it may be Dr. Gerrard. Bob is inclined to agree. They have not gone too far when suddenly Bob says

Dr. Gerrard (Christopher Lee) gives a sedative to Penny Appleby (Susan Strasberg) in a deceptive scene from *Taste of Fear* (1961).

that he sees Jane standing alongside the road overlooking the sea. Her car is parked nearby. Bob tells Penny that they will have to stop and give Jane some explanation. Penny protests that they should keep driving. Bob counters by saying it's too late. Jane will have recognized the car.

Bob stops and gets out. He begins talking to Jane. Suddenly the car starts to slide heading for a cliff overlooking the ocean. Penny in desperation tries to reach out for the wheel from the back seat. As she does so, she sees her father's corpse in the front seat. She screams as the car plunges over the cliff and smashes on the rocks below.

Bob and Jane embrace. It is they who have plotted not only to kill Penny's father but to do away with Penny herself, making Jane the sole heir. Their story will be that Penny's father wanted to take her for a ride and the car went out of control, fell off the cliff and killed them both.

In the police station, Jane and Bob tell this story. Jane is advised that her husband's attorney is arriving from England to go over the affairs of the estate. She prepares to go home but the police want Bob to go with them to the scene of the accident for identification purposes. After both Jane and Bob have left, the police inspector opens a door to an adjoining room and out steps Dr. Gerrard. He has obviously been listening to all that has happened.

Several strange things begin to happen to both Jane and Bob. At the scene of the accident, Bob is informed that only one body, the father's, has been found. Penny's body seems to have disappeared. Back at the house, Jane tells the lawyer about the deaths of her husband and Penny. The lawyer responds that this could not have been the case since Penny had died in a drowning accident in Switzerland two weeks earlier. Jane is visibly shaken by this news.

Jane learns that a young woman in a wheelchair is perched on the cliff overlooking the sea at the back of the house. Jane goes to investigate and is shocked to find Penny, safe and sound. Only it isn't Penny: The woman is actually Penny's close friend Maggie Freeman. It was Penny who drowned herself in Switzerland, not Maggie. Maggie had called Penny's father that night with the news. When a letter arrived purportedly written by Penny's father inviting Penny to come home, Maggie realized that something was wrong since Penny's father knew that she was dead. Maggie then got in touch with Dr. Gerrard and together they planned to thwart the murderous plans of Bob and Jane. Maggie, an able-bodied woman and an accomplished swimmer, was able to escape from the car before it plunged over the cliff.

Together Maggie and Dr. Gerrard have caught Jane and Bob. Maggie also reveals that the police now know everything. She walks back into the house. Jane, overcome, sits in the wheelchair, her back to the house. Bob has just returned after having heard about the young woman sitting in the wheelchair overlooking the cliff. Thinking this is Penny, Bob runs up behind her and pushes her off the cliff. Jane falls to her death. Dr. Gerrard comforts Maggie.

Key Themes

Taste of Fear has a double surprise ending. The first reveals the deadly plot of Jane and Bob to kill Penny and her father. The second is the counterplot woven by Maggie-Penny and Dr. Gerrard. The idea of a multiple twist ending is not new but it had been widely popularized by *Les Diaboliques* and by Hitchcock's *Psycho*. However, these comparisons aside, *Taste of Fear* can stand on its own merits. Jimmy Sangster would exploit this "twist ending" effect in several more films for Hammer (*Maniac, Paranoiac, Nightmare*).

The surprise effect is the point of the film, and as long as the audience can't guess the outcome before the key revelation at the end, the film can be said to be a success. The real test is the question of whether the film's premise can really hold up under scrutiny. In many respects, *Taste of Fear* does hold up. We can trace back the steps of Jane and Bob fairly easily. They make an effort to frighten "Penny" while at the same time pretending to be helpful. Jane's warning to Penny about not getting too close to Bob is a particularly effective device since it would only seem to lead Penny to depend on him more, thereby making her more vulnerable.

The counterplot of Maggie and Dr. Gerrard, as enticing as it is, is less effective once analyzed. Granted, films of this nature don't depend on internal logic and coherence to be effective; but the film's overall success still rests on how believable it all is. This is where *Taste of Fear* has some drawbacks (not to say that *Les Diaboliques* and *Psycho* don't also have a few holes). The biggest stumbling block: Why doesn't Jane know that Penny is dead from the outset? Given that Maggie called to tell the father of his daughter's death, wouldn't he share that news with his wife immediately? At that point, the only person Jane needs to eliminate in order to inherit everything is her husband. All she and Bob would have had to do would be to kill him and then send him in a car off the cliff by himself.

The other difficulty is the partnership between Dr. Gerrard and Maggie. Yes, they could have laid out their basic plan over the phone, but once Maggie was on the scene, wouldn't they have to communicate? Maggie is still taking a great risk getting into the back seat of a car that will soon be going over a cliff. Is Dr. Gerrard aware of this? Is there any way they could have been in touch with each other without arousing suspicion? It would seem that the two of them would have had to have been in some communication once in Nice. One wonders how they were able to work together, especially in the homestretch.

But despite these rather significant weaknesses, the film overall is tense and exciting and its basic premise of the hunted trapping the hunters is certainly effective.

Christopher Lee as Dr. Gerrard

Lee thought very highly of this film. Even though he is a supporting character (as he was in many Hammer films), he is still very effective. Lee really plays a double role and, in spite of his limited screen time, he is essentially successful in both parts of his character. At first, he presents Dr. Gerrard as a classic red herring. He seems suspicious but does nothing inappropriate. He gives "Penny" a medication to help her sleep after her first traumatic encounter with the corpse (this would have to have been unsettling even for Maggie in her play-acting role). His questions at a later dinner about "Penny" having another examination of her disability is also appropriate although Lee gives his performance a slight undercurrent of menace. Again, in the context of the plot within the plot, had Gerrard and Maggie somehow rehearsed this scene?

Lee essentially is inviting us, the audience, to think we see through his feigned suspicious character. When Penny-Maggie speculates for Bob's benefit that she thinks perhaps Jane's accomplice is Dr. Gerrard, we are inclined to believe her. At the same time, the more seasoned filmgoer would think this too obvious and really suspect that Gerrard is just a red herring.

What most viewers would not be prepared for is the fact that he really is a heroic figure, working undercover both to protect Maggie (though it's not totally clear how he is able to do that) and bring the murderers to justice. More than being a red herring, Gerrard is acting in disguise. He appears at first to be allied with Jane but that is far from the case. In his most effective scene, he emerges from behind the closed door in the police inspector's office. There is a look of determination on his face as his tall figure appears out of the shadows. In retrospect, he is revealing himself as the avenger of Penny's father's murder.

This is as close as Lee ever came to playing Sherlock Holmes for Hammer. A disguise such as this, with the intention of capturing the murderers in the act, is very much a Holmes trait. The more elaborate the deception, the more it echoes the scheme to catch the criminals unaware. One is reminded of Holmes' famous line, "I am Sherlock Holmes. It is my business to know things other people don't." There is certainly a trace of this in his comforting of Maggie at the end. He is revealed as having been in charge in many ways. It is unfortunate that Lee would play Holmes several times (as we will see in a later chapter) but never for Hammer. He comes the closest here.

5

The Terror
of the Tongs (1961)

The Context of the Film

By the early 1960s, Hammer was beginning to expand their themes and subjects. They had built an international reputation redoing classic Gothic horror subjects. *Time* magazine did a story on them as they were in production on *The Mummy*. Hammer had just released *The Hound of the Baskervilles*, which *Time* described as "a fresh and frightening look" at the Sherlock Holmes classic. By 1961, in addition to *The Mummy* and *The Hound of the Baskervilles*, they had also released *The Curse of Frankenstein, Dracula (Horror of Dracula), The Revenge of Frankenstein, The Man Who Could Cheat Death, The Brides of Dracula, The Two Faces of Dr. Jekyll (House of Fright)* and *The Curse of the Werewolf.* Following the success of Alfred Hitchcock's *Psycho,* they began a series of black-and-white suspense thrillers, the first (*Taste of Fear*) with Christopher Lee in a supporting role. They later produced a number of costume adventure films, two of which (*The Devil-Ship Pirates* and *The Pirates of Blood River*) had Lee in major roles.

Hammer's output had always been eclectic. They had established themselves with mystery thrillers and adventure films years before they began their cycle of Gothic horrors. What was different by 1960 was that Hammer had an international star team in Peter Cushing and Lee. Whereas their earlier mystery and even science fiction films depended on American character actors to boost box office appeal, they now had Cushing and Lee to entice audiences.

It is in this context that we need to review a Christopher Lee film that is not as familiar as it should be: *The Terror of the Tongs,* filmed in color but released in the United States in black and white. Its importance lies in the fact that it brings together a group of classic film genres: Gothic horror, exotic adventure, spy thriller and even gangster. For purposes of the present study, it is also important to note that it is the first Hammer film to give Christopher Lee top billing. This was the era of which Martin Scorsese said, "[I]f we saw the logo of Hammer Films we knew it would be a very special picture" (quoted on the back cover of *Hammer House of Horror: Behind the Screams* by Howard Maxford). Lee had played title characters in *Dracula* and *The Mummy* but top billing always went to Cushing, who initially was a far more familiar name, at least in Britain, due to his Shakespearean roles and his television work. By 1961 a legion of fans knew the name of Christopher Lee. He had become a star in his own right.

The Film

In 1910 Hong Kong, residents live in fear of a powerful secret society known only as the Red Dragon Tong. The society, which supposedly has its base in mainland China, practices extortion and exploitation through nefarious means such as drugs and prostitution. People are afraid to acknowledge

Lee as evil Chinese overlord Chung King, with accomplices Roger Delgado and Geoffrey Toone, in *The Terror of the Tongs* (1961).

the existence of the group, much less testify about their activities. The ultimate weapon of the group is their practice of ritual murder which they carry out in full public view, showing both their disdain for the police and their confidence that they can keep the populace intimidated through fear. These "sacrifices" are carried out by heavily drugged followers who use an ax as their weapon of death and who are not afraid to die themselves. (Despite its age, this film has a contemporary feel to it, especially with the present reality of Isis and our fear of terrorist attacks.) The leader of the society is a man named Chung King, played—not surprisingly—by Lee.

Given its period, this is Hong Kong as a fully British colony. A British shipping agent, Jefferson Sale (Geoffrey Toone), is only slightly aware of the fact that there is a secret movement which calls themselves the "liberators" and are pledged to overthrow the Red Tong. Sale comes in contact with a man named Ming (Burt Kwouk), whom we are to learn is part of the liberation movement. Ming has a secret document listing the names of the members of the secret Tong society. Ming knows he is a marked man since the Tongs are desperately seeking to retrieve that list and have learned that possesses it. He hides it in a book which he gives to Sale ostensibly as a gift for Sale's grown daughter (Barbra Brown).

Ming is the victim of a ritual slaying when a drugged man attacks him with an axe. A bystander who claims to be a doctor seems to come to his aid but in reality gives him a deadly injection which kills him. Ming's home is ransacked by the Tongs. Their leader, Chung King, is prepared to do whatever is necessary to find the list.

Sale gives his daughter the book, which neither of them knows contains the list. Sale also gives her a ring. There is a tender scene between them. The Tongs trace the list to the book and, while Sale is out, they break in, kill his daughter and take the list which is subsequently given to Chung King, who burns it. He regrets the death of Sale's daughter, not because of any real concern for her, but only because it may lead to complications.

The girl's death has a devastating impact on her father. From this point forward he pledges to seek out and destroy his daughter's murderers. This of course brings him into conflict with the Red Dragon Tong society. The police warn him not to get involved in something he knows nothing about, but he is undeterred. He seeks out any person who can give him information. Sale speaks to an elderly Chinese woman (Marie Burkes) who admits knowledge of the Tong but doesn't have the courage to talk about them. Sale's actions come to the attention of a street beggar (Marne Maitland) who in reality is one of the leaders of the "liberation" movement. The elderly woman invites Sale back at a time when one of the extortionists working for the Tongs (Ewen

Solon) is due to come and collect the "'protection money" which the woman is forced to pay weekly. The man is accompanied by Lee, a glamorous Eurasian (Yvonne Molnear, the beautiful French teacher in 1960's *The Brides of Dracula*).

Sale, realizing what this "protection money" is, fights with the man. He pulls a gun on Sale only to be knocked unconscious by Lee. She later explains to Sale that she was the operative's virtual slave and was looking for a means of escape. From this point forward, she wants to be Sale's companion. He resists but only to a point. Her beauty is enhanced throughout the film by the vivid dresses that she sports. In their discussion of what is taking place with the Red Dragon Tong, complete with all its vices (even white slavery), Lee comments that, as an Asian, "We can't be English." China represents a whole different way of life.

Sale's activities come to the attention of Chung King and his advisors, including some British subjects who have sided with the dangerous but very profitable Tongs. Sale, given his status, represents a definite threat to the Tongs, who thrive on a combination of secrecy and intimidation. Sale is lured into one of the Tong strongholds where opium and prostitution are very evident (somewhat surprising given the censorship in both England and the U.S. at the time). Sale is drugged and then finds himself in the clutches of Chung King. King demands that Sale reveal all that he has learned. Sale refuses. King then calls on his chief torturer (Milton Reid), a hefty bald figure who is prepared to scrape Sale's bones. King takes delight in pointing out to Sale how painful this will be. It is indeed painful to the point where Sale passes out. He is placed in a room until he revives. The leader of the liberation movement who has been disguised as a beggar frees him and returns him to his home.

King decides that allowing Sale to live is too dangerous. The doctor (Charles Lloyd-Pack) who killed Ming is sent to kill Sale. Lee does not see through the deception and, thinking the man to be a doctor sent to help Sale, allows him into the bedroom. Once alone inside, the doctor prepares a fatal injection. Sale awakes just as the doctor bends over him with the needle. In the struggle, the doctor is killed. King decides to forego any further subtle attempts to murder Sale or to try and extract information from him. The decision is made to kill him as one of the Tong's "ritual sacrifices." This will be a public death and a warning to any others who might try and follow Sale's example.

A plan is hatched to lure Sale to the docks. The liberationists see this as a moment when they can lead an all-out attack on the Tongs. Sale understands that it is a trap but realizes this may be a last chance to confront the Tongs.

Hopefully the citizens of Hong Kong will be inspired to join them and finally end the threat of the Red Dragon Tong. King has discussed his plans with Harcourt (Brian Worth), one of the English members of the Tong. The ritual involves a night of unrestrained pleasure. The man selected to kill Sale is accompanied by two prostitutes and will have his fill of opium. When he awakes, he will still be under the drug's influence which will give him the strength to accost Sale in public with the deadly Tong ax.

Lee, concerned for Sale's safety, follows him to the docks. At 10 pm Sale is on the docks. There are plenty of people present. The assassin races out of the shadow screaming and holding the ax aloft. Sale shoots him several times but, in his drugged state, the man keeps coming. Lee rushes to Sale, and the man plunges the ax into her back. She dies, having saved Sale's life. The leader of the liberationists calls out to the crowd to rise up and join them to overthrow the tyranny and fear of the Red Dragon Tong. They all do so.

Harcourt, observing all this, rushes to King and tells him that there is a massive revolt taking place against the Tongs and that the crowd will soon be at his door. Harcourt knows that now is the time to flee and he demands payment for his services as a Tong spy. We of course realize what the outcome of his demand will be and he is quickly put to death. In a moment, the liberationists and Sale break into the headquarters of King. He realizes that all is lost and instructs the advisor to stab him in the back, in effect committing suicide. He asks his ancestors to look favorably on him and collapses in death.

On the surface *Terror of the Tongs* can appear to be another example of melodrama similar to scores of other films, but it is much more than this. Its use of character, context and theme transcends its somewhat simple plot structure. To appreciate its full impact, we need to look at it in a broader context.

The Terror of the Tongs is not fundamentally an adventure film even though it has elements of that. In fact, one could argue that Hammer's adventure films (which continued to be part of the company's output after the successes of their Gothic horror films) were, like their mystery suspense thrillers, clearly influenced by the emphasis on horror. A clear example of that was a 1959 film which also dealt with a terrorist cult in a context of British colonialism, *The Stranglers of Bombey*. It's no *Gunga Din* or *The Four Feathers*. Directed by Terence Fisher, who up to this point had directed virtually all the Hammer Horrors, it had horrors of its own. Granted there were no vampires or monsters in the film. Yet tortures abound. Hands are chopped off. Eyes are put out. There is a dark, sensuous but deadly beauty as well as a cobra, both of which the hero (Guy Rolfe) has to overcome in order to survive.

There are certainly Gothic moments in *Tongs*. The ax murders are bloody and graphic. There is the torture sequence of Sale having his bones scraped. The death of his daughter is disturbing. She also is a blood victim. The fact that most of the murders are presented as ritual sacrifices adds another spiritual or even supernatural element.

Peter Cushing's Van Helsing described Dracula and his followers as a cult. The Tong followers are not only criminals. They are disciples of evil. There is a recurring emphasis throughout the film regarding the nature of the Tongs. They traffic in drugs, prostitution, gambling, embezzlement and extortion. Yet, more than this, they delight in sadism and cruelty. From Lee's all-in-black malevolent leader to the doctor who kills rather than cures, to its focus on instilling fear, the whole essence of the Tongs represents a world in darkness.

Yet this film cannot be considered just another Hammer Horror any more than it can be simply labeled an adventure film. The film has an intriguing standing in cinema history. It points both backwards and forwards. It emerges at a time when film is about to begin to undergo significant changes both with regard to film themes and the treatment of those themes, In terms of the past, the film, on at least one level, follows the conventions of the classic gangster film. This portrayal of Hong Kong could easily be adapted to Chicago in the 1920s. It doesn't take much to imagine the Red Dragon Tong as a crime syndicate. Instead of Lee's Chinese overlord, one could easily imagine an Al Capone or some other gang leader presiding over his empire. Instead of opium, there would be alcohol. Gambling and prostitution would be part of the equation. Ordinary people forced to pay protection money to the syndicate would be essentially the same. Respectable citizens who actually collaborate with the gangsters are also part of the scene. The police are helpless or, worse, on the take. The situation needs an unusual hero like an Eliot Ness (or a Jackson Sale) to stand up to the fear and corruption.

The classic gangster film was hardly absent from the context in which *Tongs* was filmed. Beginning in 1959, in the United States at least, there was the television show *The Untouchables*. These implacable government agents famously took whatever steps were necessary to bring down Al Capone and a host of other 1930s criminals. The reaction to this enormously popular series was not unlike the reaction to many of the Hammer films. The show was considered too violent. It had too much sex. Yet *The Untouchables'* success could well have been a factor in depicting a criminal empire such as we find in *Tongs*.

It could be argued that *Tongs* also incorporates some elements of *film noir*. In Fritz Lang's classic *The Big Heat* (1953), police detective Glenn Ford investigates a crime syndicate. The syndicate plants a bomb in his car. However, his wife gets into the car before he does. She is blown up and killed. The detective declares one-man war against the murderers. He has to deal with his own police department which includes both corruption and cowardice. The detective, after many trials, is finally successful. In a sadistic moment, one of the gangsters throws hot coffee into a woman's face, scarring her. She returns the favor by doing the same to him at the end.

Another feature of the gangster film is the fear of "the other." One of the objections to the *Untouchables* TV show was that the criminals were overwhelmingly Italian. There was of course an element of truth to this beginning with Al Capone himself. In the series, the Mafia was shown to have their own ritual killings, complete with a special ceremony focusing on the one who had been chosen to commit the murder, such as the "kiss of death." At several points in *Tongs* there are discussions about the differences between "Occidentals" and Chinese. Lee's aforementioned comment is one example but there are several others. The British ostensibly are in charge. However, they are shown to be dealing with behaviors and traditions that they don't really understand.

This brings up the issue of colonialism which functions in this film as well as *Stranglers of Bombay* and a host of others. The 1960s saw the rise of concerns about colonialism in a number of cases including books like Franz Fanon's *The Wretched of the Earth,* films like *The Battle of Algiers* and the Vietnam War. This period also saw the emergence of African nations from under the shadow of European colonialism. The issue of colonialism in a film like *Terror of the Tongs* is treated in a mixed way. On the surface the British are seen as necessary to oppose a terrorist sect like the Tongs. Yet we are shown British leaders who are corrupt. A protest like "We can't be English" resonates throughout he film. If nothing else, the film seems to be aware of the underlying issue. It is not simply bad Chinese vs. good Britons like a variation on cowboys and Indians. This film, and *Stranglers,* operate within the context of British colonialism and indeed imperialism. This is clear enough in the painfully obvious fact that many of the Chinese characters, including Chung King, are played by English actors in Asian makeup. Looking at the larger context of the 1960s, including Christopher Lee's own career, shows how the British colonial ideal, while being questioned, was far from dead.

A year after *Tongs'* release, one of the biggest franchises in film history began. James Bond first appeared on screen in 1962's *Dr. No.* Bond, the ultimate British colonial hero, represented a revival of the "sun will never set" view of the British Empire. Bond went through film after film saving not only the British Empire but the world (one of his antagonists in a later film was

Lee as the Man with the Golden Gun). Bond often acted alone. He could be ruthless. He was up against secret terrorist organizations like SPECTRE. He was usually in the company of a beautiful woman who oftentimes worked with his opponents but invariably came over to his side (e.g. *Goldfinger*). It doesn't take much imagination to see a corollary between Jefferson Sale and James Bond. Bond simply extends and elaborates on a figure like Sale.

There can be no discussion of British colonial influences without acknowledging the pervasive and very destructive issue of racism. *Tongs* propagates the longstanding view of the Yellow Peril, the late nineteenth and twentieth century perception that the Chinese were out to take over the world and the only thing standing in their way usually was a British leader. We may discuss the positive and negative influences of colonialism as an example of good vs. evil in these films. Yet often at the heart of the matter is an essential definition of good vs. evil in racist terms, simply put, white (good) vs. non-white (evil). The fact that these issues are so current makes it imperative that we look at the roots and earlier expressions of these views since they are still so prevalent.

This film was the first time in Lee's career that he played a completely evil, virtually all-powerful Chinese figure. Four years later, he embarked on a virtual career playing Sax Rohmer's Chinese super-villain, Dr. Fu Manchu. The virtual embodiment of the Yellow Peril, Fu Manchu appeared in a series of novels that lasted from before World War I right up to World War II. His Sherlock Holmes–type nemesis was Sir Nayland Smith, whose friend Dr. Petrie was a surrogate Dr. Watson. Formidable and frightening, Fu Manchu really is the first pop culture super-villain. At the end of each novel, his mad plans to conquer the world would be thwarted. Yet he was never really defeated. Lee's Chung King has more than a few overtones of Dr. Fu Manchu. It therefore was no surprise when Lee began a series of Fu Manchu films in 1965. This was also the year in which U.S. troops were significantly built up to face a form of "Yellow Peril" in the Vietnam War. (Racism is inevitable in any war but it should be noted that the Vietnamese were often given derogatory names like "gooks.") Lee played Fu Manchu five times on screen, his second most filmed character, after Dracula.

The many film incarnations of Dr. Fu Manchu have to be seen as antecedents to *Terror of the Tongs*. One of the most notable of these was the 1932 MGM production *The Mask of Fu Manchu* starring Boris Karloff as Fu Manchu. Viewed today, the film is either hilarious or depressing depending on your perspective. It is outrageously racist. At one point, Fu Manchu asks his followers, "Do you want white women? Then kill the white man and take his women." The flip side of this was Fu Manchu's sexy but deadly daughter, played by Myrna Loy in Asian makeup.

Another notable example of the Yellow Peril was the immensely popular Flash Gordon movie serials, from 1936 to 1940. Flash's outer space villain was Ming the Merciless who, with his slanty eyes and thin mustache and beard, was Fu Manchu in everything but name. He lusts after the blonde Dale Arden while his dark, sultry daughter tries to entice Flash.

There are key issues of good vs. evil and even of revenge vs. justice in *Terror of the Tongs*, as well as key aspects of Lee's performance that need to be discussed. However before doing so we need to acknowledge that the racist stereotype at the center of the film and of Lee's performance is a major defect that undermines the film as a whole In spite of this defect, *Tongs* presents key issues that have been part not only of cinema but of art and philosophy in general.

The nature of evil is a deathless topic. The Red Dragon Tongs are symbolic of the character of evil itself. Evil is not just an individual manifestation of a particular figure whether that is Chung King in this film, Count Dracula, Professor Moriarty or the Devil himself. Evil is a system. It is a network. The image of secret societies and crime syndicates testify to this basic fact. When evil is reduced to a specific figure or a single act, its larger nature is overlooked. This is not to minimize the impact of individual figures but even the Devil himself has a retinue of demons and evil spirits as part of his ultimate spiritual empire of evil.

Tongs is not alone in depicting this network of evil. But the film presents the classic view in very direct and clear terms. While not a great film, its portrayal of evil is easily seen. Evil operates in the film in two fundamental ways. The first is seduction. The Tongs society offers pleasure in very real but deadly terms. This is seen in the film in terms of the reality of opium, symbolic of any form of drug dependency. The second clearly is prostitution. This is shown in remarkably vivid forms for a 1961 English-language film (European films particularly at this time were far more frank and explicit than films made in Britain or the U.S.). Chung King speaks freely of acquiring "new girls" and offers them to his English collaborators. The final enticement of the Tongs evil is gambling and we are reminded time and again throughout the film that "the house wins." It could not be otherwise. The seductive aspects of evil culminate in the preparation for the man who is scheduled to be Sale's executioner. Prior to carrying out his assignment, he is sent off with two prostitutes and a store of opium to have what King calls "the most pleasurable night of his miserable life."

One can say all this is all so familiar as to be a cliché. But as familiar as it may be, the clarity and simplicity with which it is presented is more effective than many films that strive for some more philosophic understanding of evil.

The idea that the power of evil ultimately lies in seduction is clear in the Bible. The serpent in the Garden of Eden does not attempt to frighten Eve. He offers the forbidden fruit to her as a "delight." Hammer's top director, Terence Fisher, said in an interview that if the apple had been moldy with worms crawling out of it, there would have been no temptation. The offer of opium or prostitutes in no way includes the consequences of drug addiction or venereal disease. The parallel text in the New Testament to the temptation in the Garden of Eden is Jesus' temptation in the wilderness. Again, the Devil here seeks to seduce, not intimidate. The Devil suggests that Jesus, after fasting for 40 days, turn stones into bread to satisfy his hunger. When this fails, the Devil proceeds to offer Jesus "all the kingdoms of the world and their splendor" (Matthew 4:8). The evocative term "splendor" conjures up the image of every conceivable form of pleasure. Satan makes the offer not only of pleasure but of power, fame and wealth. As is made clear in this film and many others, these offers either prove false or come with very negative consequences.

Seduction is the first strategy of evil but it is hardly the only one. If the Devil's first offer of pleasure fails, his next course of action is instilling fear. We see this clearly in the film. The general populace who may or may not frequent the dens and club which the Tongs support are forced to pay "protection." Otherwise they face the destruction of their homes and businesses. The ritual slayings of the Tongs, deliberately carried out in public, are intended to intimidate and frighten the onlookers. The message is clear. The person who dares to oppose the Tongs will meet the same fate. Again this is consistent with the Biblical picture of evil. Demons can destroy those who oppose them.. There are numerous examples of people who are demon-possessed and who are therefore the subject of violent attacks. In one vivid example, a distressed father tells Jesus that the demon that has entered his son throws him into fire and water (Matthew 17:15). *Tongs* shows similar forms of violence intended to overwhelm any opposition. The combination of seduction and fear is central to the character of evil. Those who join terrorist groups are first enticed by promises of power and success. In the end, they resort to attacks which are designed to inculcate fear. This combination (seduction followed by fear) is inimical to the whole character of evil. The fact that we can find this depicted in a popular film like *Terror of the Tongs* makes the message no less significant.

A related issue we see in the film is the whole question of revenge vs. justice. This issue goes all the way back to the ancient Greeks. Jefferson Sale at the start of the film is largely indifferent to the cruelty and corruption of the Tongs. This all changes when his daughter is brutally murdered. He becomes obsessed with finding her killers. He refuses to listen to the police (a not unreasonable attitude given their ineffectiveness and possible collaboration with the Tongs). His intense focus also leads to his becoming foolhardy. Entering one of the many dens of the Tongs, he accepts a drink which even we the audience are not surprised to learn is drugged. In the course of all this, Sale almost loses his life. In the climax, he comes close to dying at the hands of the assassin who has been groomed to kill him. He is saved when Lee intervenes and takes the ax blow that was intended for him (This also is classic film morality of the period. As enticing and appealing as Lee is, she is fundamentally a prostitute and therefore has to suffer the fate of all "bad girls").

Sale forces himself to learn as much as he can about the Tongs following his daughter's murder. He sees the injustice and corruption of the society. Yet we are left with the clear impression that, had his daughter not been killed, he might have remained largely indifferent to their activities. He is outraged when he discovers that one of his allies, a Chinese woman, is forced to make payments to the Tongs if her little shop is to be allowed to continue to operate. We are however left with the question, is Sale responding to the injustice he sees or are his actions based on a quest for revenge? Obviously the two are not mutually exclusive. But one can wonder, what is the primary motivation here, vengeance or justice?

As noted, this is an issue that the Greeks dealt with in depth. Following the brutal killing of his cousin, Patroclus, at the hands of Hector in the Trojan War, Achilles embarks on a campaign of vengeance. There is a justice issue here since Patroclus had surrendered to Hector and was unarmed, seeking to retreat when Hector killed him. Achilles' response descends into savagery as he now proceeds to kill unarmed Trojans. After finally defeating and killing Hector, he drags his body around the city walls of Troy. Homer, writing in *The Iliad,* calls this a "shameful outrage." It is clear that Achilles is acting far more out of revenge than anything else. The same applies to the classic story of Orestes who murders his mother and her lover following their murder of his father, Agamemnon. Different Greek authors view Orestes' actions either as just or merely based on revenge, depending on their point of view.

This issue is still very much with us. In the classic film *Taken,* a father searches for his kidnapped daughter. He is not above using torture to get the information he needs. Most Americans were gratified when Osama bin Ladin was killed. Again, was this a just sentence or an act of revenge motivated by the carnage of 9/11? We clearly sympathize with Sale in the film, especially after seeing the tender relationship he has with his daughter. His subsequent actions seem primarily to be motivated by revenge. Yet the film is clearly asking us to sympathize with him. In the course of events, he recognizes the injustice of the Tongs. The film never really asks us to determine to what extent his actions are justified. The picture follows a standard narrative outline which never really stops to ask larger questions. However, this cannot be dismissed as, "Oh, it's just a movie." The ancient stories of Achilles, Orestes and other heroes were the popular stories of their time. The nature of the storytelling itself lends itself to these questions. These questions will not go away.

Christopher Lee as Chung King

We have already seen the racist element of having the diabolical Chinese mastermind portrayed by Western actors in makeup. Even acknowledging that drawback, we nonetheless can see that Lee here gives a remarkable picture of evil and his portrayal merits consideration. Lee's characterization of Chung King conveys overtones of Satan himself. This is seen in Lee's black clothing. He is cultured, well-spoken, intensely rational and supremely calculating. King really is evil incarnate. His only desire is for power and control and he will do anything to maintain that power. He uses drugs, sex, intimidation and torture to accomplish his ends. What are those ends? Presumably they are nothing less than complete control of Hong Kong. This includes mastery over the police as well as British government representatives.

Chung King is not only Lee's first starring role, it is a departure from his earlier Hammer portrayals which themselves were often essays in evil. Chung King, however, is not only an evil figure. He is evil incarnate and it is a credit to Lee's performance that he does not degenerate into caricature. The Creature in *The Curse of Frankenstein* was, as discussed earlier, an abused child, more a victim than anything else. Even Dracula, described as the most evil person who ever lived, has a motivation of self-preservation. Dracula drinks the blood of his victims not simply to attack and dominate them but also to preserve his own life. As the Bible bluntly states, "For the life of the flesh is in the blood" (Leviticus 17:11), a verse which Bela Lugosi's Dracula memorably echoes, "The blood is life." This is hardly to say that Dracula is a sympathetic character. But his actions are motivated in part by a desire to prolong his own life, a desire that obviously is shared by all of us.

Lee's portrayal of the Mummy invites sympathy. Kharis the Egyptian high priest who becomes a living mummy is motivated by his love for the Princess Ananka. There is an essential sadness about him when he confronts the image of his long-lost love. Even Lord Summerisle in *The Wicker Man* is seeking in his bizarre way to benefit his community by offering a sacrifice so that the crops will grow. In a supporting role in *The Two Faces of Dr. Jekyll,* Lee portrays Jekyll's close friend Paul, who is having an affair with his Jekyll's wife and, at the same time, is constantly asking him for money. Paul accompanies Mr. Hyde on his nightly excursions around London, but he recoils at Hyde's violence. A weak, self-serving figure, Paul gets his comeuppance at the end of the film. His forays into evil don't compare to those of Mr. Hyde.

Chung King outdoes all of these characters. He asks for no sympathy. He delights only in power and domination. There are no boundaries to what he will do to gain that domination. When he tells Sale that his daughter's death was "regrettable," he is showing no degree of sympathy. His comment works on two levels. He professes this small amount of concern only because he wants information from Sale. Second, the girl's death is only regrettable due to the fact that it complicates his plans (the murder of a British subject is more likely to trigger an investigation than the death of one of the locals).

King speaks only in icy, menacing tones. There is no cordial, "I am Dracula and I welcome you to my house." King cares for no one. Even his allies are expendable, as he shows more than once. He has no life beyond his leading the Red Dragon Tong. When he is confronted with the certain overthrow of his empire, he asks his associate to kill him. King's only interest seems to be power. He has no trace of humanity. Such a character could be simply one-dimensional, but Lee creates a character that fascinates us at the same time he repels us. We are impressed with his cold, calculating, authoritarian manner. Watching Lee give this dark performance is like watching a snake, both frightening and somehow appealing. Chung King is not often listed among his best roles. This is unfortunate since Lee rises above the racial stereotype implicit in the character to create a dark, foreboding presence. There is probably no more sinister portrayal in the extensive film career of Christopher Lee than Chung King.

6

Christopher Lee on Baker Street

Christopher Lee has the notable distinction of having played three different characters from Sir Arthur Conan Doyle's Sherlock Holmes stories. He has played Holmes himself on three occasions. The first was a German film directed by Hammer's Terence Fisher, *Sherlock Holmes and the Deadly Necklace*. Many years later he played the part of Holmes in two made-for-television movies. He also played Holmes' brother Mycroft in Billy Wilder's *Private life of Sherlock Holmes*.

However before essaying any of these parts, he was cast as Sir Henry Baskerville in Hammer's landmark version of *The Hound of the Baskervilles*.

The Hound of the Baskervilles *(1959)*

Following the global success of Hammer's initial Frankenstein and Dracula films, Universal gave the studio access to all the film fright characters it had under copyright, including the Mummy, the Wolf Man and the Phantom of the Opera. Robert Louis Stevenson's much filmed *Dr. Jekyll and Mr. Hyde* was in the public domain by the late 1950s. Plans were made to film all of these including even a new version of Robin Hood (Hammer had made *Men of Sherwood Forest* in 1954 in color).

But before any of these went before the cameras, Hammer chose as its next production an adaptation of the classic Sherlock Holmes novel *The Hound of the Baskervilles*. Even though on an initial level this was a detective story, it also qualified as a tale of terror. The mystery Holmes is called in to solve deals with a ghostly hell hound which has haunted the Baskerville family for centuries. Holmes and Watson here are confronted with a problem which appears to be supernatural in character. In a famous line from the novel, Holmes says, "In a modest way I have combated evil, but to take on the Father of Evil himself would, perhaps, be too ambitious a task." Hammer then saw the relation of Holmes to the Hound as somewhat similar to Van Helsing's conflict with Dracula. In addition, the setting of the story was the fogbound moors of Devonshire. This would then be Hammer's first Gothic Horror film set in their native England. Plans were then made to bring together the same team that had done the Frankenstein and Dracula pictures, headed again by director Terence Fisher. The cast would feature the essential duo of Peter Cushing and Lee.

It was no surprise that Cushing was cast as Sherlock Holmes. His thin frame, piercing eyes and prominent nose made him ideal for the part. In addition, he was a longtime Holmes enthusiast. He therefore insisted on the proper clothes, pipes and even dialogue not only from *The Hound of the Baskervilles* but from other Conan

Lee as Sir Henry Baskerville in *The Hound of the Baskervilles* (1959).

Doyle stories as well (In response to a question about his fee, Cushing quotes from the story "The Problem of Thor Bridge": "My professional charges are on a fixed scale. I never vary them save when I remit them altogether."

Cushing played the role of Holmes numerous times, including a BBC-TV series in 1968 and a 1984 TV movie entitled *The Masks of Death*. The part of Dr. Watson went to veteran character actor Andre Morell. The same year as *Hound*, 1959, Morell appeared in the Oscar-winning film *Ben-Hur*. He had also previously appeared in 1957's *The Bridge on the River Kwai,* which won the Best Picture Oscar that year.

Lee was given the part of Sir Henry Baskerville, the last heir of the estate and a future victim of the hell hound. In the many versions of this story, Sir Henry is usually portrayed as a young, likable figure who tends to dismiss the story of the Hound as nothing more than a superstition. This was the approach of young British actor Richard Greene in the classic 1939 Hollywood version in which Greene got top billing over Basil Rathbone (Holmes) and Nigel Bruce (Watson).

One of the problems of portraying Sir Henry is the nature of his relationship with Beryl Stapleton, with whom he falls in love. Beryl is ostensibly the sister of Jack Stapleton, a naturalist and scientist who lives on the moor. In reality, Beryl is his wife and he is actually also a Baskerville. His birth was unknown to the rest of the family since his father had died in Costa Rica. In the novel, Stapleton has brought the hound of legend to life by acquiring a large, savage dog whom he treats with a mixture of phosphorus so that it appears to glow with hellfire. In this elaborate plot, Stapleton's wife is forced to pose as his sister so that she can lure Sir Henry out onto the moor alone where he can be killed by the hound. Stapleton and his wife would then return to Costa Rica and seek the estate through the British consulate there under their real name of Baskerville, with no one realizing that they were the Stapletons living on the moor close to Baskerville Hall.

In the novel, Beryl at first tries to warn Sir Henry without implicating her husband. She refuses at the end to carry out the murderous seduction. The reason for this is her discovery that her husband has been having an affair with another woman, a woman who lured Sir Henry's uncle out onto the moors at night to face the hound. Beryl then is no ordinary woman. She is described as "one of the beauties of Costa Rica." Her hair is darker than that of any woman in England. She is further described as being both beautiful and exotic. While Sir Henry genuinely falls in love with her, he is unaware that he is being led into a deadly trap.

Most portrayals of Beryl avoid the complexity of her character. She is usually portrayed by an English actress. Watson's description of her as "a most uncommon type" is usually ignored. In some versions such as the 1939 classic, she is totally unaware of what, in this film, her "stepbrother" is up to. By making Beryl such an unusual figure Conan Doyle introduced a latent subtext of foreign, albeit very appealing, sexuality. This is heightened by the fact that Stapleton clearly wants to use her as bait but doesn't want Sir Henry to actually make love to her. Hammer's version of this relationship, while not exactly that of the novel, is more faithful to the spirit of the book than most other film dramatizations.

In the story, Holmes and Watson are introduced to the mystery by a Dr. Mortimer who, following the strange death of Sir Charles Baskerville, is concerned about the fate of Sir Henry, the last known living heir. While Holmes expresses his skepticism about the hound and the curse on the family, he agrees to meet Sir Henry. Our first picture of Sir Henry shows him putting the finishing touches of his morning preparation in front of a mirror. Before uttering any dialogue, Lee has established the character as aloof, privileged and aristocratic, all this by simply showing how he finishes dressing himself in front of a mirror. Holmes and Watson knock and are invited into his room. Assuming without asking that Holmes is the hotel manager, he berates him over the loss of one of his boots (a key clue in the story). Dr. Mortimer soon enters and makes the formal introductions.

In this opening sequence, Lee establishes Sir Henry as more than a conventional figure. Hammer's films have been cited as depicting important class distinctions with an essentially negative view of those who benefit by such distinctions. Dracula is a noble, a count. Sir Hugo Baskerville in the opening sequence of this film is sadistic and self-indulgent. Lee captures the image of a wealthy aristocrat who is used to giving orders and having his way. Our initial reaction to him is to be put off to some degree. This changes when Sir Henry takes hold of the remaining boot and a tarantula emerges and begins crawling up his arm. He looks terrified. Lee in interviews has maintained that it was a real tarantula and his frightened appearance was more than acting. Holmes manages to kill the tarantula. As a result of this episode, we are more inclined to be sympathetic to Sir Henry.

Peter Cushing as Sherlock Holmes (left) shakes hands with Christopher Lee as Sir Henry Baskerville with Francis De Wolff (Dr. Mortimer) and Andre Morell (Dr. Watson) looking on in *The Hound of the Baskervilles* (1959).

Holmes believes that Sir Henry is in real danger. However he claims not to be able to leave London at this time and suggests that Watson accompany Sir Henry home and help protect him. At this point the story as well as the film focuses on Sir Henry and Watson's experiences at Baskerville Hall and on the moor. Lee is able to capture both the somewhat aloof character of the aristocrat along with his obvious intention to be a good host to Watson and to interact with members of the community. There is a brooding sense of something malevolent. It is not only the hound but the whole atmosphere of Dartmoor, coupled with the news that a Jack the Ripper–type killer has recently escaped from prison and is hiding out on the moor. As a horror story, the emphasis here is on atmosphere and the dread of something evil.

The critical dimension of Sir Henry's situation arises from his encounter, in this version, with Stapleton's daughter. Several things need to be noted here. First, Cecile (instead of Beryl for some reason) is Hispanic and is the exotic beauty of the novel. She fears her father, whom we will learn is plotting against Sir Henry with the hound. Second, the obstacle to a marriage between her and Sir Henry is not the fact that she is Stapleton's wife as in the novel (and no doubt the British censor in 1959 would not have permitted such a marital deception). The obstacle here is one of class. The Stapletons are essentially peasants. There is no way that someone from their class could marry an aristocrat like Sir Henry, especially in Victorian England. Cecille also in this case is fully involved in the plot to kill Sir Henry. There is no possibility of an unfaithful spouse since the Stapletons here are father and daughter rather than husband and wife.

Cecile suddenly kisses Sir Henry when they first meet outside Baskerville Hall. He goes to the Stapleton cottage where they embrace and kiss again, only to be interrupted by the entrance of her father. The father doesn't mind since this is all part of the plot. We see that Sir Henry's interest in her is more of a clandestine nature than a straightforward romance that could lead to marriage. Sir Henry is enjoying the benefits of a beautiful woman. There is no question of love here. But Lee instills in Sir Henry's character a basic decency seen in his treatment of the other characters. Sir Henry has a temper and has an altercation with Dr. Mortimer, but he keeps Sir Henry likable throughout. He is not perfect but he is essentially good-hearted.

Holmes arrives on the scene to provoke a climax. In an evocative sequence, Holmes, Dr. Mortimer and Stapleton, go into an abandoned tin mine where Holmes suspects the hound is kept. A car on the rails in the tunnel threatens to come loose so Mortimer and Stapleton hold it in place, allowing Holmes to go further down into the mine. The car comes loose and as a result Holmes' leg is injured. That night, Sir Henry, Holmes and Watson are invited to dinner at the Stapleton home. Stapleton wants to encourage frequent visits on Sir Henry's part since this requires Sir Henry to cross the dark and foggy moor to get to their home. Sir Henry comes to Holmes and Watson's room and sits down with them. He proceeds to tell them of the invitation to dine at the home of the Stapletons. He is obviously torn by what he sees as his duty to his guest, who obviously can't go to the dinner, and his desire to be with Cecile.

Holmes, sensing all this, deliberately provokes Sir Henry by referring to the Stapletons as peasants in a derogatory manner. Sir Henry promptly rises to his feet. Fisher makes this even more dramatic by shooting Lee's action from a low camera angle. Sir Henry makes it clear that he vehemently resents Holmes' comments. He storms out of the room and, as we will see, into the deadly arms of Cecile. Lee here shows Sir Henry at his best. He clearly is an aristocrat and is used to having a privileged position. On the other hand, he has a sense of basic decency and fair play. In his mind, the Stapletons, while of a different class, nonetheless should be treated with respect and dignity. At this point, we can only applaud him.

In the next scene, we see Sir Henry is a much darker vein. He is walking with Cecile alone back to her house. She lures him into the dark old abbey where his notorious ancestor, Sir Hugo, was killed by the hound. In this final sequence, we see the talents of set designer Bernard Robinson and photographer Jack Asher. The foggy ruins of the abbey are as desolate and menacing a locale as one could imagine. But Sir Henry sees it only as a remote spot where he can enjoy the benefits of Cecile. He kisses and caresses her. She steps away and he follows, seeking to kiss her again. She suddenly slaps him and identifies herself as a member of a Baskerville clan that was forced to live in poverty while, in her words, "you scum ruled the moor." While Sir Henry did not force her into poverty (this evidently went back several generations), he is trying to take advantage of her. Given his social status, his actions cannot be called honorable.

Yet whatever misgivings we may have about Sir Henry's actions, we instantly become sympathetic to him when Cecile virtually spits out the words, "The curse of the hound is upon you!" The howl of the hound is heard as Sir Henry, bewildered and terrified, looks all around him. This is the one major misstep of the film: Instead of seeing a ferocious beast, all we are given is the image of a shadowy great dane perched above Sir Henry. The hound attacks Sir Henry. In the melee, Holmes and Watson shoot the beast, which turns on Stapleton. (The hound actually bit Lee and he had to be taken briefly to a hospital. The bite was not serious.)

Dr. Watson (Andre Morell, left) steadies Sir Henry Baskerville (Christopher Lee) after he's been attacked by the demonic Hound. Holmes (Peter Cushing) shows the boot that gave the Hound Sir Henry's scent.

Sir Henry has to be helped up by Holmes and Watson after the hound's death. Its corpse (with blood-stained teeth) looks more frightening than it did alive. Sir Henry's clothes are torn and his face has bloody scratches from his ordeal. As Holmes and Watson help him walk back to Baskerville Hall, they see Cecile caught in the mire, being sucked down to her death. The closing scene of the film has Holmes and Watson receiving a missing portrait of Sir Hugo (along with a generous check). Lee's voice is heard reading the thank you note to Holmes. After all the harrowing events, the film closes with a cozy scene of Holmes and Watson having tea at Baker Street.

There is a growing critical consensus that Hammer's version of the *Hound* is the best of the many versions. One Hammer documentary calls it the company's most accomplished film. There are many reasons for this, beginning with Cushing's superb performance as Holmes and Andre Morell's excellent Watson. What is often overlooked is Lee's outstanding performance as Sir Henry. The part is often done as little more than a two-dimensional character at best. Sir Henry really is just the foil around which the legendary hound and the rest of the cast rotate. Lee's Sir Henry is a more complex character. He has both positive and negative qualities. He can appear as an entitled aristocrat as well as someone who can be a sympathetic host, a supporter of local charities (in his scene with the eccentric Bishop Franklin, played by Miles Malleson) and, to a degree, a supporter of the rights of others as he defends the Stapletons against Holmes' intentionally derogatory remarks.

He is made more sympathetic by his obvious vulnerability. He has a heart condition which opens up the possibility that the hound could be used to frighten him to death as had been the case with his uncle. He easily falls into traps (the tarantula and the hound itself). The most obvious trap for him is Cecile. She is the closest film incarnation of the "tropical and exotic" beauty described in the novel. Hammer's reducing the Stapletons to peasant status removes the possibility of any socially legitimate (by Victorian standards) relationship between them. The fact that Sir Henry foolishly wants to arrange a clandestine meeting with her on the moor at night sets him up for his encounter with the hound. Yet we never lose our sympathy for him. We are left with the impression, as is the case in the original novel, that he has learned a hard lesson from having been seduced by her.

In short, Lee's portrayal of Sir Henry is one of his best parts in any Hammer film. His Sir Henry is a more complex figure than we find in any of the other versions of the story.

The Private Life of Sherlock Holmes *(1970)*

For many years, the great German immigrant director, Billy Wilder, wanted to make a Sherlock Holmes film. Wilder's impressive film credits include *The Lost Weekend, Sunset Blvd., The Seven Year Itch, Some Like it Hot* and the Academy Award–winning *The Apartment*. He had apparently read the Holmes stories in translation as a boy in his native Germany and had never lost his interest in them. With his screenwriter collaborator I.A.L. Diamond, he hoped to do a four-part film which would run over three hours. Budget concerns reduced the film to essentially a prologue with only one of the four parts included.

The film opens in the modern day, borrowing from the story "The Problem of Thor Bridge" which states that Watson has a tin box in the vault of the bank Cox and Company which contains accounts of cases that were never published. The film purports to be one of those although it clearly has echoes of the first Holmes short story, "A Scandal in Bohemia."

In that story, to the dismay of many readers, Holmes is outwitted by a woman who is described as an "adventuress" of dubious and questionable memory. The woman's name, familiar to any Holmes fan, is Irene Adler; she is an American (from New Jersey no less) and an accomplished singer. The fact that Watson insists that Holmes had no romantic feelings for her and that by the time of the story she is dead, has not stopped endless speculation that she somehow was the love of Holmes' life.

This really is the focus of Wilder's film: Did Holmes ever have any affection for a woman? William Gillette, who both wrote and starred in the first Sherlock Holmes dramatization, famously asked Conan Doyle if he could have Holmes marry in his play. His equally famous response: "You can marry or murder or do whatever you like with him." The result of this was that Holmes clearly falls in love with his client, Alice Faulkner, a character not found in any of Conan Doyle's stories. It is hard for modern Holmes fans to picture such a love affair on the part of the great detective. Yet up until Basil Rathbone's Holmes films, the beloved Alice Faulkner appeared frequently. John Barrymore's film *Sherlock Holmes* (1922) ends with her in the detective's arms. A Holmes film ten years later shows her engaged to Holmes and having to be rescued from Moriarity.

The whole question of Holmes' relationship with women recurs throughout Wilder's film. Wilder has Holmes and Watson played by two British stage actors, Robert Stephens and Colin Blakely, respectively. In an early sequence, a Russian ballerina suggests that she and Holmes have a child together, combining her beauty with his brains. He begs off, giving her the impression that he is gay and in a relationship with Watson, much to Watson's horror.

The film focuses on a beautiful Belgian woman who shows up at Holmes' 221-B address having lost her memory. Eventually she claims to recover her memory. Now Gabrielle Valladon (Genevieve Page) wants Holmes to help her find her missing husband. Holmes follows a trail that leads to Scotland. It is at this point that Christopher Lee enters.

Lee here plays Holmes' brilliant brother Mycroft. In the few Conan Doyle stories in which Mycroft appears, he is described as corpulent and utterly resistant to physical activity. He has a position at the highest level in the British government; Sherlock says that Mycroft, in effect, *is* the British government. Lee's appearance is totally different. He is tall, thin and bald.

Mycroft both resents and admires his brother, whom he describes as the greatest mind in England. Mycroft reveals a shocking truth: Holmes' client,

Mycroft Holmes (Christopher Lee) challenges his brother Sherlock (Robert Stephens) in *The Private Life of Sherlock Holmes* (1970).

whom we have seen is getting more and more attention from him, is, in fact, a German spy. Her made-up story was designed to entice Holmes to take her to a secret location where Britain is experimenting with the idea of a submarine. The submarine has been disguised as the Loch Ness Monster. Mycroft points out that not only has Holmes been duped but he has been working with an enemy of his country. Throughout their travels, they have been followed by what appears to be a group of Trappist monks. The monks are in fact other German spies. Gabrielle, whose real name is Ilsa von Hoffmansthal, has been communicating using Morse code by opening and closing her parasol.

Lee's Mycroft is in sharp contrast to his brother. Robert Stephens' Holmes is something of a romantic. Given the fact that he has been tricked, he has nonetheless operated out of a desire to rescue a woman in distress. Even knowing of her deception, he still appears to be attracted to her. Mycroft is both a cynic and a realist. If England doesn't develop a submarine, her enemies will. In any event, war will be the inevitable outcome and England must prepare.

Queen Victoria comes to view the secret location where the submarine is being developed. Mycroft takes great delight in describing what an effective weapon of war it would be. He proudly states that it will be able to sneak up undetected on ships and blow them out of the water. The queen is horrified by the idea of such a weapon and wants it destroyed. Mycroft is forced to comply.

Mycroft has the idea of a parting shot in which he enlists Sherlock's aid. The spies pretending to be monks are allowed to steal inside the submarine. However an explosion has been planned which destroys both the submarine and the spies. It appears initially that Gabrielle (Ilsa) will be executed as a spy. But, in an almost weary tone, Mycroft says that will not be the case since she will be traded for one of Britain's spies in German custody. As she is being taken away in a carriage, she uses her parasol to give Holmes a final "auf Wiedersehen." Subsequently, Holmes receives a note in Baker Street from Mycroft telling him that Ilsa was sent to Japan as a spy and was discovered and executed. Holmes is clearly affected by the news. He takes his cocaine and retreats to his bedroom as the film ends.

Lee's Mycroft is very much of a counterpoint to Sherlock. He seems to relish the fact that Sherlock has been completely duped to the point of actually aiding German spies. Lee's Mycroft is very much of an example of *realpolitik*. His focus is on what is practical and expedient. Sherlock, on the other hand, tries always to pursue the good and the true. Lee's Mycroft clearly plays up the idea of a rivalry between the two brothers. Yet Lee's sending Sherlock the notice of Ilsa's death shows he has a measure of concern, if not outright sympathy, for Sherlock. Ilsa is not important to Mycroft as a person; he sees her as little more than a commodity to be exchanged for one of England's spies. He gives her a backhanded compliment by saying that he doesn't think England is getting the best of the exchange.

In an interview, Lee said that Wilder was the best director he ever worked with. That's not surprising given Wilder's record. Many would rate this film as one of the most original and effective Holmes films of all time. While there is much to admire about it, Lee's portrayal of Mycroft plays into a diminished view of Sherlock. Granted, Wilder wanted to explore Sherlock's relation to the opposite sex and he does succeed in showing Holmes caring for Ilsa to some degree. But this is at the expense of what we would expect from Sherlock Holmes. Do we really think that this group of Trappist monks following Holmes, Watson and Ilsa would fool, in Mycroft's mocking phrase, "the best brain in England"? Won't Holmes realize that Ilsa was using her parasol to send Morse code messages to her fellow spies? Lee's Mycroft plays into this mocking picture of Sherlock, leaving the impression that while this film has an affectionate view of Holmes, it is also a sardonic one.

Sherlock Holmes and the Deadly Necklace *(1962)*

This film is the first of three times that Lee actually played the Great Detective. Following his success in Hammer Films and several films Lee had done on the continent, he was offered an intriguing opportunity: to play Sherlock Holmes in a German-made film with an English actor as Watson (Thorley Walters, who went on to appear in a number of Hammer films, including Lee's *Dracula, Prince of Darkness*) as well as a British director, Hammer veteran Terence Fisher. Screenwriter Curt Siodmak was German but had scripted a number of Hollywood horror films in the 1940s such as *Frankenstein Meets the Wolf Man, I Walked with a Zombie, Son of Dracula* and *The Beast with Five Fingers*. Given such a team, there were high hopes for this production. The film was to be released in both a German and an English version (Lee spoke German).

For reasons which are unclear, the film was released to the English-speaking world with Lee's voice dubbed by an unknown actor. In addition, Lee appears as Holmes with an unnecessary and even distracting fake nose. The music for the film seems completely inappropriate. The film has to be relegated to the category of a "might have been."

In many ways, Lee would make a fine Holmes. His tall, lean and penetrating eyes and distinctive voice all contribute to the image of Holmes. One notable aspect of the production is that it gave Lee the opportunity to meet Sir Arthur Conan Doyle's son Adrian. This reinforces Lee's connections with the famous inhabitant of 221-B Baker Street.

The film is uneven and may be missing sequences. It had no theatrical release in the U.S.; there it went straight to television at the end of the '60s. The story is roughly based on Conan Doyle's Holmes tale "The Valley of Fear." This is mixed in with an account of Professor Moriarty stealing Cleopatra's necklace. Holmes retrieves it by breaking into Moriarty's home in disguise. Moriarty is bent on regaining it, which accounts for much of the film's action. Interspersed with the Holmes-Moriarty conflict is a murder scene (taken from "The Valley of Fear") involving a victim whose face has been shot off.

Lee strides through this rambling film looking impressive even *with* a fake nose. But it is impossible to evaluate his performance without being able to hear his voice. What does come across is the heroic character of Holmes.

Dr. Watson (Thorley Walters, left) confers with Sherlock Holmes (Christopher Lee) in *Sherlock Holmes and the Deadly Necklace* (1962).

As in the original novel, Scotland Yard does not believe Moriarty is "the Napoleon of crime" that Holmes claims he is. While Holmes retrieves the necklace he is unable to link its theft to Moriarty. In the presence of police Inspector Cooper, Holmes seeks to show that Moriarty's cane contains a sword. Moriarty earlier had attacked Holmes with this sword-cane. However at this moment, Moriarty reveals that the cane contains only a small flask of brandy. This is one of the few films where Moriarty goes scot free at the end. Worse, he is pursuing a Texas millionaire who has just purchased the necklace at an auction.

Lee brings a brooding intensity to the role. His face expresses defiance when told by Inspector Cooper to leave the "innocent" professor alone. When checkmated by Moriarty at the end of the film, Holmes expresses a resolute intention to continue his battle with the mastermind of crime. The most important point to be gleaned from this admittedly frustrating film is that Holmes intends to do right whether or not he is believed and whether or not he is successful. Lee's Holmes may face setbacks but he will never admit defeat. That point alone gives the film some merit.

Sherlock Holmes and the Leading Lady *(1991)* and Incident at Victoria Falls *(1991)*

In 1990, Lee agreed to appear in a series of made-for-TV cable films as Sherlock Holmes. Veteran actor Patrick Macnee, most famous for his role in the TV series *The Avengers,* would play Dr. Watson. There were significant problems with these productions.

First of all, Lee at 68 was a retirement age Sherlock Holmes. He could hardly handle the excessive physical action that defined Holmes as a sportsman and that Peter Cushing exemplified so well in the role. Second, the films were set around 1910 by which time, according to Watson in the Conan Doyle stories, Holmes had been retired for seven years, keeping bees in Sussex. The films were the brainchild of producer Harry Alan Towers, who had cast Lee in a series of lurid Dr. Fu Manchu films.

The two Holmes telefilms were made in Luxembourg. The first was directed by former Hammer director Peter Sasdy (*Taste the Blood of Dracula, Countess Dracula*), the second by Bill Corcoran who directed a number of TV films (*Web of Deceit, The Girl Had Two Lives*). Each film ran 175 minutes.

To put it bluntly, neither film was a distinguished production. The stories were so lengthy and complicated, they were difficult to follow. At nearly three hours, it was also hard to maintain interest. Efforts were made to establish an impressive setting, Vienna in the first film and South Africa in the second. Adding to the confusion: the introduction of real-life figures Sigmund Freud, Austrian Emperor Franz Joseph and U.S. Prohibition agent Eliot Ness (who was a child in 1910) in the first film and Theodore Roosevelt in the second. The fact that this historical figures are somehow tied in with Holmes makes nonsense of the standard credit line that "no actual persons real or intended" are referred to in the film. The famous fictional thief Raffles also appears in the second film. The "leading lady" of the first film is none other than Irene Adler, portrayed by the glamorous Morgan Fairchild. Her relationship to Holmes is one of the genuinely intriguing parts of these lengthy productions. However, given the fact that she was 28 years younger than Lee at the time of production, she gave the impression of being his daughter rather than his equal.

Despite these drawbacks, the films offer a sustained picture of Lee's portrayal of Holmes even in advanced age. (It was not helpful that these productions had to compete with the Jeremy Brett Holmes episodes which were well established on both sides of the Atlantic by the early 1990s.) Lee's Holmes benefits from both his height and his imposing voice. Lee is like a coiled spring threatening to break out at any moment. When Mycroft comes to tell him that the empire is at stake, he responds with diffidence. There are too many other important things competing for his time. But when Mycroft insists that Holmes is needed not only for England's sake but for the whole of Europe, Lee's facial expression alters just enough to catch the image of a knight errant who realizes he must ride to the rescue. Lee makes superb use of his hand gestures and his eyes. On at least one occasion, he raises his index finger to make a point, a familiar gesture of his frequent co-star, Peter Cushing.

There is a certain surreal character to these films due in part to their merging of the mythical and the historical. Fairchild's Irene Adler has been asked by the emperor to sing in the Richard Strauss opera *Die Fledermaus*. This is occasioned by her wearing a bat gown that more than a little suggests the comic book Batgirl. What focus the films are able to maintain comes from Lee's brooding and intense performance. To watch him in the role is to wish he had been given the opportunity to play the character in a major production decades earlier.

Lee does bring an important new dimension to the character of Holmes, at least in the first film *Sherlock Holmes and the Leading Lady*. He explores not only Holmes' alleged interest in Irene Adler but his attitude to women in general. There is an impressive scene in a ballroom where Irene wants him to dance with her. He declines, saying, in effect, that dancing and the arts in general simply don't suit him. Irene will not take no for an answer. She insists and so he attempt to dance with her. He conveys the impression of a man who is so focused on being in charge of himself that he will not allow any possible distraction. This includes any full emotional expression.

There is a scene with Holmes and Irene dining together in her room. She has cooked the meal. Once again she asks Holmes to dance with her. She puts on a phonograph record to give them some music. Holmes is clearly attracted to her. He is at the point of kissing her but pulls himself away. There is something of the priest in Lee's portrayal. In a somewhat veiled but clear way, he confides to her that in order to maintain the concentration required for his work, he cannot indulge in any intimacy. This picks up and complements the earlier dance sequence mentioned above. Holmes needs to be completely in charge of himself, not because he is self-absorbed but because he essentially has a mission to fulfill. Yes, he seeks to escape boredom through solving crimes. But there is more to it than that. As we saw in the opening sequence, he was inclined to dismiss Mycroft's entreaty because he presumably did not find it interesting. However once Mycroft had communicated the gravity of the situation, Sherlock rose to the occasion.

For all the weaknesses of these two overlong films, they do bring up the theme in Watson's words from "The Final Problem" that Holmes is the best and wisest man he has ever known. In these films, Holmes does more than uncover a criminal. He manages to prevent the world from plunging into war (at least for the moment). He therefore needs to focus all his attention on the problems, indeed crises, that are presented to him. While Irene is very appealing, she can have no place in the kind of life to which he has dedicated himself. She alludes to this fact by raising the question: What will the world do when Sherlock Holmes is no longer present? She speculates that the only way to continue Holmes' legacy is for him to have a son. Her meaning is clear. (William Gillette's play *Sherlock Holmes*, which first appeared in 1899 and was enormously popular for decades, shows Holmes falling in love with his client Alice Faulkner. However Conan Doyle himself never presented Holmes in a romantic relationship.)

Lee offers a valuable interpretation. He brings a clear moral tone to Sherlock Holmes. Holmes is far more than a reasoning machine, a solver of puzzles and crimes. He is finally a force for good in a broken world. In the story "The Blue Carbuncle," Holmes speaks of saving a soul. Christopher Lee's Holmes comes close to saving the world.

7

Rasputin
the Mad Monk (1966)

Upon its initial release, *Rasputin the Mad Monk* was largely dismissed by critics who noted that, while it was based on a historical character, it was largely fiction. Some were impressed by Christopher Lee's performance but most saw it as an unsuccessful attempt to vary Hammer's basic horror film approach. While the film can certainly be called a Hammer Horror, it nonetheless adds new dimensions to Hammer's standard formula. The film is ripe for reappraisal not least because it contains one of Lee's best performances and its focus on good vs. evil forecasts later Hammer films such as *The Devil Rides Out*.

Context of the Film

In 1963, Hammer was at a crossroads, and seeking new directions. They released a big-budget (for Hammer) version of *The Phantom of the Opera*, which was a disappointment because it emerged more as a love story than an out-and-out horror film. Some critics scoffed at the Phantom whose face, when finally revealed, was hardly frightening. In reality, Hammer's prime director Terence Fisher had in fact captured the romantic essence of the original story which decades later proved so successful on Broadway.

For the time being, however, Fisher was on the outs with Hammer and spent the next year making films for other companies, including an unsuccessful horror spoof called *The Horror of It All* starring singer Pat Boone, no less. Hammer had already branched out into costume adventures, some of which had starred Lee (*The Pirates of Blood River, The Devil-Ship Pirates*), as well as black-and-white thrillers which were too obviously attempts to imitate the success of Alfred Hitchcock's *Psycho*. Columbia, which had distributed a number of Hammer's films in the U.S., were becoming increasingly dissatisfied. Earlier films such as *Never Take Sweets from a Stranger* and *The Two Faces of Dr. Jekyll*, while worthy films in their own right, were judged too extreme for the period, the former being a striking account of child abuse. Columbia was unhappy with both films. The subsequent Hammer films that Columbia released were hardly the box office draws that the earlier Frankenstein and Dracula films had been. Hammer's one Frankenstein film in this period, *The Evil of Frankenstein,* released through Universal, was also a disappointment, its monster being a weak imitation of the Boris Karloff version.

Hammer was still being run by James Carreras and his son, Michael. They had not lost their knack for innovation or showmanship. The first step in revitalizing the Hammer formula was to bring Terence Fisher back and reunite him with Peter Cushing and Lee. The resulting film was the dark and moody *The Gorgon,* based on a character out of Greek mythology. Aside from some disappointing special effects, this is one of Hammer's most atmospheric and intriguing films. Released in the fall of 1964, it set the stage for Hammer's rebirth in 1965.

The Gorgon was the blueprint for Hammer's revival. This consisted of drawing on Hammer's earlier successes and aligning them with intriguing new properties. These innovations also included a stronger sexual element, given the more open atmosphere of the mid–60s and the success of the James Bond films. While this did not include nudity at this point, it did allow for stronger sexual content. The results were dramatic. Hammer signed a new distribution agreement with Twentieth Century-Fox and created the production company "Hammer-Seven Arts." The first film released under this logo was a suspense thriller that was closer to actual horror. Hammer brought back its earlier practice of starring former Hollywood character actors in key roles. The result was *Fanatic* (U.S. title, *Die! Die! My Darling!*) starring well-known Hollywood film actress Tallulah Bankhead. The cast also included Stefanie Powers and Donald Sutherland in early roles. This was followed by no one less than Bette Davis in one of Hammer's most accomplished thrillers, *The Nanny.*

Hammer also combined Cushing, Lee and the first James Bond girl, Ursula Andress, in an elaborate film version of H. Rider Haggard's adventure fantasy *She.* This formula led to their most financially successful film up to that point, *One Million Years B.C,.* starring Raquel Welch. Veteran special effects director Ray Harryhausen supplied what was for that time superb dinosaur effects. Plans were also made to bring Lee back as Dracula (in the previously discussed *Dracula, Prince of Darkness*). Hammer also laid plans for a zombie film (*The Plague of the Zombies*) and, in another variation on *The Gorgon,* a film about a snake woman, *The Reptile.*

Hammer now began filming two pictures with essentially the same cast, crew and settings. This was not only an economy measure but it also laid the groundwork for several double features that could play in major theaters throughout Britain and the U.S. All of these elements are important to note since they have a direct bearing on *Rasputin the Mad Monk.*

Rasputin the Mad Monk *(1966)*

One of the bright spots of 1963 for Hammer was the vampire film *The Kiss of the Vampire.* It was directed by Don Sharp, who went on to become one of Hammer's most accomplished directors; Sharp was at the helm of *Rasputin the Mad Monk.* He had previously directed Lee in Hammer's *The Devil-Ship Pirates* and in two of producer Harry Alan Towers' Fu Manchu films. One of the criticisms of *Rasputin* was that Sharp tried to make a historical subject into a Hammer Horror.

Rasputin the Mad Monk drew on all the themes that Hammer was treating as of 1965. It had elements of horror but in other ways it was a costume drama. It had a historical premise but was essentially a fictionalized story. It was arguably also a religious film and a suspense thriller, and it included sexual themes. The film was shot right after *Dracula, Prince of Darkness* and featured many of the same cast and crew members. Set-wise, Castle Dracula became Rasputin's villa. Hammer had the foresight not to release two such matching films on the same program. *Rasputin* was paired with *The Reptile* while the Dracula film double-billed with *Plague of the Zombies.*

The preparation for the film could not ignore some of the genuine historical issues involved in the story. In particular, the real-life assassin of Rasputin, Prince Felix Youssoupoff, was still alive at the time of the film's production. In 1965 he was in the process of suing CBS for how his wife was depicted in *If I Should Die,* a television drama dealing with the same incidents. His suit was unsuccessful but it gave Hammer pause while it was pending. In the film, Youssoupoff's character becomes the fictional Ivan (Francis Matthews). The ambiguous character of the real-life Rasputin had inspired other films, most notably MGM's *Rasputin and the Empress* (1932) starring his brother John Barrymore as Rasputin and sister Ethel.

The real life Grigori Efimovitich Rasputin was born in 1871 and, as in the film, exercised major influence over the czarina of Russia. He was assassinated in 1916 on the eve of the Russian Revolution. Lee did some research, as he had done for *Dracula.* But *Rasputin the Mad Monk* never purported to be historically accurate. Before we can fully appraise this unusual film, we have to look at its actual content. There are a number of familiar Hammer motifs in it, but they are not simply echoes of earlier films. They are part of a genuinely innovative film.

The Story of the Film

Rasputin the Mad Monk opens as many Hammer films do, in an isolated inn. The innkeeper is distraught because his wife has a high fever. A doctor says he can do nothing. All of a sudden, a towering figure enters the inn: the monk, Rasputin. In a domineering voice, he calls for the landlord. He is told by those in the inn that the landlord is unavailable because he is caring for his wife. Rasputin makes his way into the woman's bedroom and claims that he can bring the fever out of her. He touches her face with his hands and soon the woman recovers. Overjoyed, the innkeeper asks how he can repay the monk. Rasputin responds that he can do so by supplying him with wine.

There is a celebration at the inn with Rasputin drinking and dancing. As the festivities continue, Rasputin takes a young woman outside to a stable. They lie down in the hay and he kisses her passionately. Her boyfriend suddenly appears and attacks Rasputin. The two fight. The boyfriend has Rasputin on his back but Rasputin manages to grab a sharp scythe and proceeds to cut the young man's hand off. We see the hand fall onto a pile of hay. This was taken at the time as an obligatory nod to Hammer's horror tradition. The girl is shocked. When Rasputin tries to force himself on her, she screams. Several inn patrons enter and there is a brief scuffle with Rasputin until he leaves.

In the next scene, Rasputin is being questioned by his bishop. The severed hand, in a grisly touch, is on the bishop's desk. Rasputin claims he was acting in self-defense (which in a purely literal sense is true); the bishop seems more concerned with Rasputin's drinking and womanizing. Rasputin defends himself by saying that when he goes to confession, he wants to have some sins that are really worth confessing! The bishop is appalled by this attitude. The bishop's attention is then drawn to the fact that Rasputin healed a woman that the doctor could not cure. The bishop says that such a gift would not be given by God to someone as sinful and rebellious as Rasputin. He then concludes that this power must have come from the Devil. Rasputin says, "The power is mine and I shall use it as I please."

Rasputin next gets into a drinking bout with a disgraced doctor named Boris Zargo (Richard Pasco). He moves into Zargo's home in St. Petersburg. One night in a tavern, Rasputin encounters two men who are accompanied by their sisters. As Rasputin drinks and then dances, he imagines the women are laughing at him. He is particularly annoyed at the woman named Sonia (Barbara Shelley, the First Lady of Hammer Horror). He demands an apology and almost gets into a fight with her brother Peter (Dinsdale Landen). Rasputin leaves, still insisting on the apology.

Sonia in her bed overhears Rasputin's demands. In the morning she returns to the tavern to ask about Rasputin. The owner, absorbed in his morning paper, tells her where he lives but adds, "Be careful." Sonia replies that she can take care of herself. If only she knew.

She comes to Boris and Rasputin's home and apologizes as requested. Rasputin sends Boris out for food and drink and then proceeds to seduce Sonia. His tearing off her skirt and grasping her bare back sets the tone for the stronger sexual content of this film. Soon the two of them are in bed together. Rasputin has learned that Sonia and her attractive sister Vanessa (Suzan Farmer) are ladies-in-waiting to the czarina. With Boris protesting, Rasputin hypnotizes Sonia and instructs her to harm the young son of the czarina but not kill him. She is then to tell the czarina that she knows of a holy man who will be able to cure the boy. When Rasputin brings her out of the trance, she appears to remember nothing.

Sonia has unconsciously retained the monk's instructions. As the little boy is playing outside the snow-covered palace (which we recognize as *Drac-*

Christopher Lee in the title role of *Rasputin the Mad Monk* (1966).

ula, Prince of Darkness' set for Castle Dracula), Sonia pushes the child off a ledge and he falls onto the frozen moat. A gamekeeper rushes to the boy's aid. Vanessa comes out of the palace and asks what happened. Sonia only says that he slipped.

The child's injuries are serious enough that the palace doctor can't help him. The czarina leads her ladies-in-waiting and servants in a prayer for the boy's recovery. Sonia, following again her hypnotic instructions, tells the czarina of the "holy man" who can cure people. The czarina sends for Rasputin, who does in fact heal the child.

Rasputin then hypnotizes the czarina and instructs her to dismiss the court physician and replace him with his friend Boris. When told of his dismissal, the court physician notes that Boris had his medical license revoked for a past "scandal." With the czarina under Rasputin's power, she can rectify Boris' situation. Boris becomes more and more concerned about Rasputin's growing power.

Rasputin has the czarina give him an elaborate villa where he and Boris can live. Rasputin is visited by many women who seek to be "cured" by him. At one point when the czarina is about to call, the women are told to leave. One protests that she has already paid for the appointment. That means little. The last woman to leave comes out of Rasputin's room trying hurriedly not only to put on her coat but seemingly to adjust her clothes suggesting what kind of "cure" Rasputin is offering these women.

Rasputin has grown tired of Sonia and, now that he has the czarina under his hypnotic spell, she is of no use to him. He tells her to leave him and never bother him again. Worse, he asks her to bring him Vanessa. Sonia goes into a rage, attacking him and telling him that she'll kill him, in one of Barbara Shelley's most impassioned scenes for Hammer. Rasputin laughs at her. He clearly maintains his dominance of her. He then hypnotizes her again, this time telling her to go and commit suicide.

Boris has reached the end of his tether. He is now convinced that Rasputin must be stopped by any means possible. He shares his concerns to Vanessa's brother, Ivan. Ivan understands the threat that Rasputin has become but he is not ready to commit murder. Boris wants to call it an "assassination." To Ivan, they are the same.

Peter, Sonia's brother, is concerned about her and goes to her apartment. The bedroom door is locked from the inside. There is no answer to Peter's calls. He pounds his fist on the door. Finally he breaks the door in, only to find Sonia's dead body on the floor. She has slit her wrists following Rasputin's last instruction to her. Convinced that Rasputin is behind her death, Peter rushes to Rasputin's home armed with a sword. The house is dark but

Rasputin is present, taunting him. In what has become in effect a laboratory for Boris, there is a vial of acid. Rasputin lures Peter into the dark lab, even telling him about the presence of the acid. We know all too well what is to occur. In the dark, Rasputin hurls the acid into Peter's face and Peter runs screaming from the house. Ivan finds Peter nearly frozen and on the brink of death outside the villa. Hearing what Rasputin has done to him, he is now prepared to join Boris in a plot to lure Rasputin to his death.

Boris wants to poison Rasputin. Ivan attempts to entice him by claiming to set up a meeting between Rasputin and Vanessa. Boris poisons the wine and a plate full of chocolates. Rasputin arrives, responding to the bait of a meeting with Vanessa. Ivan invites him to sit down and tells him that Vanessa will be coming shortly. Rasputin is left alone with the poisoned wine and candy. As anticipated, he samples both. The poison takes effect and he is in excruciating pain. He collapses on the floor. Boris runs to examine him, thinking that he is dead. That is hardly the case. In the fight that ensues, Rasputin throws a knife at Boris, injuring him. Ivan and the dying Boris thrust Rasputin out the window and he falls to his death.

Christopher Lee as Rasputin

When released, *Rasputin the Mad Monk* was dismissed as a curiosity or a hybrid, an unsuccessful attempt to merge history with Hammer Horror. Now, more than half a century later, it can be seen in a broader context. As noted above, Hammer went through a rebirth beginning in 1965. The films that are associated with that rebirth are *The Nanny, Dracula, Prince of Darkness, The Plague of the Zombies, The Reptile* and the two highly successful examples of what came to be known as "Hammer Glamour," *She* and *One Million Years B.C.* Later there would be such impressive productions as *Frankenstein Created Woman, The Devil Rides Out, Quatermass and the Pit* and *Frankenstein Must Be Destroyed.* Hammer received the Queen's Award for Industry in 1968 before the decline of the late '60s and '70s set in.

In such evaluations of Hammer's output, *Rasputin* is scarcely mentioned. This is unfortunate since the film effectively summarizes Hammer's earlier efforts and in many ways introduces its best work of the late 1960s. There are several notable things about *Rasputin* that bear mention. As far back as their first *Dracula*, Hammer had focused on the conflict between absolute good and evil. The seductive power of evil, especially in sexual terms, was present in the first installments of Dr. Frankenstein and Count Dracula. Frankenstein and Dracula in their own ways were bent on seeking power. For Frankenstein, this was the creation of life. For Dracula, it was life brought back from the dead. Religious themes and imagery were notable, especially in the Dracula films, as well as *Stranglers of Bombay* and *The Curse of the Werewolf*.

The criticism that Hammer's portrayal of Rasputin was historically inaccurate is really beside the point. The film, while drawing on the historical character of Rasputin, really uses him as a symbolic figure of absolute evil. Hammer's presentation of Rasputin, reinforced by Lee's outstanding performance, draws on two central characters, one from Greek mythology, the other from the Bible.

In the case of Greek mythology, Rasputin strongly resembles the previously mentioned Dionysus, the god of wine. He is also the god of frenzy. He draws women to himself and, under his spell, they lose all inhibitions. They are known as the Maenads. They are also accompanied by satyrs, half-human, half-goat figures reputed to have long-term erections. The rites of Dionysus (or, as he was known in Rome, Bacchus) were alleged to include orgies amid drunken revelries. Dionysus took horrible revenge on those who opposed him.

He was also a god of rebirth. He even brought his mother, Semele, back from the dead. His rebirth was associated with spring when the grapes essential to making wine became ripe. Dionysus was also the patron god of the theater. Envied and feared in ancient Greece and Rome, he could reward his followers and just as easily destroy his enemies.

Hammer's Rasputin is clearly a type of Dionysus. We see this in his enormous consumption of wine and in his revelry. Even Rasputin's dancing has a frenetic quality to it. His dominance over women is another clear parallel to Dionysus. We also see his brutal treatment of those who oppose him. His healing power suggests the power of rebirth seen in Dionysus. What Hammer did in this film, whether they were conscious of it or not, is to take the figure of Rasputin, symbolically, not literally, and cast him as a modern embodiment of Dionysus. Given what we know of the historical Rasputin, this is not too wide an interpretation. This film was made in the mid–60s with that era's emphasis on "sex, drugs and rock'n'roll," all of which are aspects of the Dionysian cult. This film taps not only into the legend of Rasputin but portrays him with clear echoes of Greek myth as well as relating him to the context in which the film was made.

The Biblical figure that Rasputin symbolizes, like Dracula, is the Anti-Christ or "the Beast." Jesus speaks of "false messiahs and false prophets" that will be able to perform "great signs and omens" (Matthew 24:24). They will lead many astray. This is where the religious content of the film becomes important. At the beginning, Rasputin's bishop says that his power must come from the Devil. The Devil is certainly able to perform acts that will deceive the inhabitants of the earth (Revelation 13:14). Moses performed miracles in Egypt but, up to a point, the magicians of Egypt were able to duplicate them (Exodus 7:14–8:7). A related figure which points up the seductive and sexual aspect of evil is "the Great Whore" who commits fornication with "the kings of the earth" (Revelation 18:3).

Rasputin's power is a warning in the continuing conflict between good and evil. Right from the start of the film, Rasputin's healing power deceives those who witness it. They give themselves over to his Dionysian celebrations of drunkenness and sex with serious consequences. Miraculous power is not necessarily from God. It can just as easily come from Satan. In that case, the value of the miracle is short-lived. Rasputin's hypnotic power will be seen again in Mocata, the satanic priest in *The Devil Rides Out.* In that film, there is no doubt that the power is demonic.

In Satan's temptations of Jesus in the Gospels, there are three basic offers. The first is to satisfy bodily desires, in this case, bread to take away Jesus' hunger. The second is to experience power. The third is actual domination (Matthew 4:1–11). Rasputin represents all of these. But those who follow him, especially Boris and Sonia, are finally destroyed by him. Therefore Rasputin is more than a "mad monk." He is more than a dark god like Dionysus. Finally he is the Anti-Christ, the direct agent of the Devil himself. Given these elements, this film deserves reconsideration as one of Hammer's most intriguing treatments of the mid–1960s.

Finally we have to discuss Lee's performance. His physical characteristics equip him well for the part. His height and booming voice already establish him as a dominant character. In the opening sequence in the inn, he emerges from the shadows in a suitably dramatic fashion. His performance really takes hold in the scene where he heals the innkeeper's wife. As a clergy person we might expect that he would respond with compassion and empathy not only for the sick woman but for her distraught family. Yet this is not Rasputin. His focus is on power, not mercy. Lee communicates right from this opening sequence that Rasputin's real desire is neither for sex nor drink. What he wants most is power. In his mind, whatever advances that power is good. This is consistent with the patterns of Dionysus and the Anti-Christ, as noted above.

Lee keeps this focus throughout the film. Sonia may be a beautiful woman but even in their initial love-making scene, Lee's focus suggests power. The intensity of the way he looks at it shows that he is mostly interested in dominating her. As the lady-in-waiting to the czarina, Sonia is a means to an end for him. Lee conveys this lust for power in all the interactions he has with the other characters. He looks down on each of them in more than just a physical way. Lee makes excellent use of his eyes, which suggest more than seeing. He uses his eyes like weapons. His looks are invariably threatening. The only thing he fears is anything that might inhibit his use of power. When he thinks Sonia is laughing at him, he is outraged. Any sort of mockery would seemingly lessen his power.

The most impressive part of Lee's characterization is the abundant pleasure he seems to feel as he works his evil designs. He laughs repeatedly in a way that can only be described as frightening. His Rasputin seems to enjoy the misery he inflicts on others. This includes such horrific examples as chopping off a hand or throwing acid into someone's face. As important as power is to him, it is in fact the pleasure he gains from inflicting pain on others that gives him greater satisfaction. He finds pleasure in belittling Boris. When Sonia expresses her rage at his decision to leave her, he laughs. He genuinely enjoys her distress,

In short, Lee's Rasputin is another highly effective portrayal of evil matching his Count Dracula and Lord Summerisle. While his acting is broad and even flamboyant, it never degenerates into pure melodrama. His Rasputin remains believable throughout. It is one of his most accomplished performances.

8

The Devil Rides Out (1968)

The Context of the Film

For a number of years, Christopher Lee had been pushing Hammer to film the novels of Dennis Wheatley. Wheatley truly was something of a pulp author whose works could hardly be called great literature. Yet he was popular, especially in Great Britain. His work focused on occult and magic themes, always with a warning to his readers to avoid any form of magic, black or white, in real life. He also infused his novels with elements of orthodox Christianity. He was scarcely in the league of a J.R.R. Tolkien, C.S. Lewis or even a Charles Williams. Yet his best novel, *The Devil Rides Out*, has to be acknowledged as a minor masterpiece of the horror genre. Hammer made a film version in 1967 with Lee in the starring role.

Hammer at this point was coming to the end of its golden age which had begun ten years earlier with *The Curse of Frankenstein*. While continuing to film Frankenstein and Dracula productions with Peter Cushing and Lee respectively, they also branched out into other areas of Gothic Horror with the previously mentioned *The Gorgon* and *Rasputin the Mad Monk* (both featuring Lee) as well as *The Plague of the Zombies* and *The Reptile*.

In 1968, *The Devil Rides Out* was a major new effort with direction by Terence Fisher and an outstanding James Bernard music score. The cast also boasted Charles Gray, an outstanding character actor who had played a villain in the James Bond films, as Mocata, the high priest of evil and magic. The movie was set in the 1920s as opposed to the usual Victorian setting of Hammer's horror films. Lee has the lead role in the film as the Duc De Richleau, one of the most fascinating characters he has ever played. De Richleau is in effect a combination of Van Helsing, Sherlock Holmes and Father Sandor.

The Film

The film opens with de Richleau (Lee) and his friend Rex Ryn (Leon Greene) preparing to visit Simon (Patrick Mower), the son of a close friend who had died in World War I. When they call on Simon, it becomes apparent to de Richleau that Simon is involved in black magic. He and Rex unintentionally interrupt a witches' gathering, becoming the fourteenth and fifteenth guests which throws off the essential number of 13. It is at this gathering that de Richleau for the first time meets Mocata (Charles Gray). There is also a young woman named Tanith (Nike Arrighi), to whom Simon is attracted.

What follows in rapid succession is a series of conflicts between de Richleau and his supporters, which include Rex, his niece Marie (Sarah Eddington) and her husband Richard (Paul Eddington), vs. Mocata and his demonic followers. Mocata is intent on bringing Simon and Tanith into their witches' coven. Rex and Richard are reluctant believers. They represent the pseudo-modern characters in many Hammer films of this period, denying the reality of the supernatural at their peril. The film is fast-paced. At one point. de Richleau and Rex rescue Simon and Tanith from a witches' sabbat where they are scheduled to be re-baptized into Satan worship. Satan himself appears in the form of a half-goat, half-human figure. The most famous scene in the film has de Richleau, Simon, Marie and Richard in a circle that is intended to protect them from the Angel of Death which Mocata is sending against them. The writing on the circle includes references to the trinity along with other symbols. De Richleau's niece's young daughter Peggy (Rosalyn Landor) is in her own bedroom guarded by the family servant. Various omens and images are invoked in order to lure the group out of the protection of the circle. These include the appearance of a giant tarantula. Each time, de Richleau pleads with Simon, his niece and nephew to stay with him in the protection of the circle. At the height of this, the Angel of Death rides in on a black winged horse. De Richleau utters a sacred incantation that, in his words, puts their very souls at risk. The incantation is successful and the Angel of Death disappears.

Their relief is short-lived: They learn to their horror that Peggy has been abducted. Tanith also has died. De Richleau is able to contact the spirit of Tanith using his niece as a medium. This is given a Christian context by his first question to the spirit: "Do you acknowledge our Lord Jesus Christ?" The spirit replies, "I do." Through the spirit, they learn Peggy's whereabouts. They arrive just as Mocata is about to sacrifice the child to the powers of evil. De Richleau, Rex and the parents are held back by Mocata's followers. De Richleau offers himself to be sacrificed in place of Peggy. Mocata snidely asks,

The spiritual warriors prepare for the coming of the Angel of Death in *The Devil Rides Out* (aka *The Devil's Bride*) (1968). From left in the circle are Paul Eddington, Sarah Lawson, Patrick Mower and Christopher Lee.

"Your soul, my lord Duc in place of that of an unstained child?" De Richleau's niece pleads with him to repeat the same incantation that sent the Angel of Death away. Yet the incantation is so powerful that de Richleau doesn't dare say it twice.

The climax is unlike anything else in Hammer or, for that matter, in horror films in general. Its striking mystical quality is underscored by Bernard's haunting score. The spirit of Tanith once again speaks through the mother Marie, giving her a striking spiritual power. Mocata and his followers draw back. Peggy, who apparently has been drugged, is revived by her mother speaking in the voice of Tanith. Peggy is told to repeat the words of the sacred incantation as Tanith speaks them. As she speaks, the Duc prays silently. Once they are spoken by Peggy, lightning strikes the altar where she was to have been sacrificed. The whole hall erupts in flames. The curtain on a back wall is burned away, revealing a cross. In the end, the hall is not only burned but purged. Mocata and his followers have simply disappeared. The group is sent back in time to earlier in the day when they had awoken from the night inside the circle. Time has been altered. In this new present, Peggy has not been abducted and Tanith has not died. Mocata however, according to de Richleau, has been taken by the Angel of Death. The rest of them are all safe. Rex simply says, "Thank God." De Richleau adds, "Yes. He is the one we must thank," as he takes Peggy up in his arms.

This film is so striking and so unusual that it could be the subject of a book-length study. It may be Hammer's finest achievement.

As for Lee's performance, it is a many-layered interpretation. The Duc de Richleau is a fascinating, multi-dimensional figure. To appreciate this fully, we need to look at the context of the film. By the time of its release in 1968, the so-called counter culture was in full force. The United States was dealing with the upheavals of the Civil Rights movement, the Vietnam War and the assassinations of Martin Luther King and Robert Kennedy. There was a generation gap between youth and their parents. This was also the era of "Swinging London." The horror film was going in new directions with titles like *Rosemary's Baby,* which also dealt with devil worship and witches' covens but in an entirely different way than *The Devil Rides Out.* Echoing the recent "Death of God" movement, the witches at the climax of *Rosemary's Baby* cry out, "God is dead! Long live Satan!"

In this context, *The Devil Rides Out,* as well as Lee's character, can seem like very conservative throwbacks to an earlier era. That however would be a mistake. Lee and his Hammer collaborators were well aware of the larger cultural setting. To appreciate this we have to examine Lee's character in detail.

Christopher Lee as the Duc de Richleau

The Duc at first glance seems to be a solitary figure. Yet while unmarried, he clearly has a family with his niece and her husband and child. In addition, Simon is a surrogate, almost adopted son. When we first encounter de Richleau, he is an anxious parent. He has discovered that Simon is engaged in witchcraft. This is an aspect of the generation gap. For many parents in 1968 seeing their children caught up in the excesses of the '60s with its "drugs, sex and rock and roll," they might as well been in a witches' coven. De Richleau then has to exercise proper authority on Simon and, later, his nephew who dismisses the idea of the supernatural entirely. On this reading, de Richleau would appear to be a conservative parent figure disciplining and correcting the younger generation. While this dimension is present, Lee makes it clear that de Richleau cares deeply for Simon. He presents himself to his niece's husband as his friend and for the sake of that friendship asks him to observe the boundaries of the circle. De Richleau is not ordering him. He is not giving him a command, playing the role of an authority figure. Instead, by appealing to him as a friend, he treats him as an equal.

Once Simon has returned to the witches, de Richleau could have taken the position that he had done all he could. He had given Simon his advice. Simon is not a child. De Richleau could have pulled back and let Simon follow his own path. Instead, he pursues Simon, at risk to himself. While he appears stern and even forceful at times, it is obvious that he is motivated by concern for his niece and nephew and his surrogate son Simon. With hindsight we can look back on the late '60s and see its dangerous excesses. For all the good accomplished in the Civil Rights movement, drugs and indulgent sex left a lot of broken dreams in their wake. It is not unreasonable that Hammer in general, and Lee in particular, shared some of these concerns.

Related to the role of the anxious and caring parent, Lee's de Richleau is also a steadfast friend. We see this in his relationship with Rex. Rex at first wants only to think of evil as an "idea." De Richleau counters that evil is a genuine, and threatening, reality. De Richleau shows his loyalty especially as Rex becomes more attracted to Tanith, who clearly is under Mocata's spell. Rather than trying to turn Rex away from Tanith, which would seem initially to be the wisest strategy, de Richleau takes on the task of rescuing her with the same energy and conviction that he is expending in trying to save Simon. As noted, he also raises the issue of friendship in his discussion with his nephew.

While these are significant aspects of de Richleau's character, and each of them is communicated by Lee in subtle ways, the dominant nature of Lee's character is his role as a spiritual warrior. This is central to his entire performance in the film. De Richleau is first and foremost an opponent of evil, evil in its most intense form. He is committed to this not only at the cost of his own life but at the cost of his soul as, for example, when he offers to take Peggy's place in a Satanic sacrifice. He establishes himself as an absolute authority in the area. This is neither a boast nor an assertion of personal dominance. De Richleau has studied the occult arts as a way of combatting the powers of darkness. His task literally is freeing people like Simon and Tanith who have been caught up in evil's web. For de Richleau, this is more than just a study. It is a lifelong calling.

In this respect, de Richleau is similar to Daniel in the Bible. Daniel and his friends are taken captive following the Babylonian conquest of Israel. Because they are young men of promise, they are placed in the king's court. We read that God gave Daniel and his three friends "knowledge and skill in every aspect of literature and wisdom" (Daniel 1:17). At the end of this period of training, Daniel and his friends are examined. We are told that they were ten times better than all the magicians and enchanters in the whole kingdom (Daniel 1:20). Daniel and his friends did not believe in the magic of Babylon, nor did they have any intention of practicing it. They nearly lost their lives because of their refusal to participate in the worship of Babylon. They mastered the magic arts of Babylon for the sole purpose of opposing it. This is the position of de Richleau. A master strategist, he even takes time out from the overt struggle to do more research. Like Daniel, his mastery of the occult and black magic is for the sole purpose of opposing and defeating it.

De Richleau lives in many ways the life of an ascetic monk. He has an impressive home. However, there is no suggestion of a romantic companion in his life. He appears to have few friends. He rejects the use of alcohol in the midst of the spiritual struggle. This too is similar to Daniel and his friends who asked to be excused from eating at the king's table in favor of eating only vegetables and water. Yet at the end of ten days, Daniel and his friends appeared "better and fatter" than those that had eaten the king's rations (Daniel 1:15). There is no suggestion in the film that de Richleau does not enjoy the finer things in life. The nature of his home testifies to this. Yet throughout all that takes place, de Richleau focuses on his mission. He will do nothing that would compromise his readiness for the spiritual battle ahead.

De Richleau is also reminiscent of the apostle Paul in the Christian New Testament. A total of 13 letters in the New Testament are attributed to Paul. He is also the central character in the Acts of the Apostles. Yet Paul frequently finds himself alone. He has an all-encompassing view of the Christian gospel which many of his fellow Christians, including the apostle Peter, don't completely share. Christianity in its early stages saw itself dependent on Judaism. Many early Christians advocated for the observance of the law of Moses, including the requirement of circumcision and the keeping of the dietary laws in the Torah.

Paul, however, emphasized that such an emphasis on the law compromised the liberating power of the gospel. Keeping the law was in reality "a different gospel" (Galatians 1:6). For Paul, this was not simply a matter of having correct religious views. He saw behind the compromised view of the gospel a Satanic influence. These were Satan's deceptions (II Corinthians 2:11). Paul saw himself in a battle against "the cosmic powers of this present darkness, against the spiritual forces of evil in the heavenly places" (Ephesians 6:12). Many times Paul saw himself fighting these battles virtually alone. When he is imprisoned in Rome and faces a hearing, not one of his followers comes to his aid with the exception of Luke, the author of both the gospel that bears his name and the Acts of the Apostles (II Timothy 4:11–16).

Similarly, de Richleau has to fight not only against the malevolence of Mocata but also overcome the doubts and uncertainties of his friends and allies.

His close friend Rex is skeptical until he is almost overpowered by the occult forces. De Richleau virtually has to restrain Richard and Marie from going out of the protective circle when confronted with the false images. At one point they think they see their daughter Peggy menaced by a giant spider; they want to rush to her aid and thereby leave the protection of the circle. Holding on to them both, de Richleau shouts, "It's not Peggy!" Eventually de Richleau's wisdom is recognized but, like the apostle Paul, he struggles alone through much of the film.

The best way to summarize de Richleau is to say that he is a combination of three major heroes in the Hammer film tradition. First is Van Helsing, who fights against Dracula and vampires in general. Van Helsing has the same intensity, ascetic lifestyle and determination in his battle with the forces of evil. The second would certainly be Sherlock Holmes (whom Lee played three times). Holmes, as portrayed by Peter Cushing in Hammer's celebrated version of *The Hound of the Baskervilles,* had a definite metaphysical if not outright spiritual character to him. Instead of saying that he is solving a murder, he tells Watson, "There is more evil around us here than I have ever seen before." Holmes certainly has the ascetic and intense characteristics that we see in de Richleau. The third example would be Father Sandor from *Dracula, Prince of Darkness.* As a priest, he has the ascetic element. He is also pledged to fight against evil and was often frustrated by those around him who did not take seriously his warnings and commands.

The Devil Rides Out was not only a major achievement for Hammer. It was, and remains to this day, one of Lee's best film portrayals.

The Wicker Man (1973)

The Context of the Film

The Wicker Man has been called the *Citizen Kane* of horror films. Additionally, Christopher Lee's performance in the film is second only to his portrayal of Count Dracula. For all the recognition the film has gotten over the years, it is striking to note that the original film produced by Lions Gate was almost lost. Lee himself helped in the preservation. In spite of a 2014 Blu-ray so-called "Final Cut," there is no totally complete version of the film, which to this day exists in multiple forms. In spite of a distinguished cast (Lee, Edward Woodward, Britt Ekland and the 1970s horror film cult figure Ingrid Pitt) and a screenplay by Anthony Shaffer who wrote the Broadway hit *Clue,* the film was not released in the United States until 1980 and even then only played in major cities. It was released to home video in multiple forms. To this day, one cannot get all the footage in a single package.

The film is a masterpiece of the genre, considered among the finest British films ever made.

The Film

In most versions, the opening scene takes place in a church in Scotland where Holy Communion is being celebrated. We are told it is April 29, 1973. A uniformed police officer (Edward Woodward) is speaking the words of institution to the Lord's Supper, blessing the bread and the wine. He is not a pastor or priest but appears to be an elder, a lay leader in the church. We see him both speaking the words of institution and also drinking the consecrated wine from a chalice as he himself receives the sacrament. We also see him in the company of the woman we will learn is his fiancée, singing the 23rd psalm along with the church congregation.

A subsequent scene (not included in the so-called Final Cut) shows this man, Sergeant Neill Howie, at the police station, possibly the following day. He receives a letter stating that a little girl named Rowan Morrison has been missing for some time on the island of Summerisle, off the Scottish coast. He determines to fly there in a boat plane to investigate. We have already learned two things about Sgt. Howie, that he is deeply and strictly religious and that he is engaged to be married. Behind his back, the other police officers mock him for what they perceive to be his prudish views.

Howie arrives on Summerisle with a picture of the missing Rowan that came with the letter. On the island, he finds himself in a surreal, and indeed decadent, world. Showing the little girl's picture to a group of fishermen on his arrival produces no results as the men deny having ever seen her. Eventually he learns that she is allegedly dead but there is no death certificate. To add to his puzzlement, he sees nudity and sexuality all around him, from bawdy songs in the pub where he has taken a room to couples having sex outdoors at night. He sees a naked woman weeping at a gravestone. Later he sees a group of naked young girls leaping over a fire in a setting that looks like Stonehenge. He goes to the home of a woman named Morrison, who claims she has no daughter named Rowan. Then he talks to the woman's little daughter privately, and according to her, Rowan does exist but now somehow lives in the form of a March Hare. The teacher at the local school, along the children, deny Rowan's existence. But in class register, Howie finds her name listed. To add to his frustration, he discovers that the children are learning about fertility rites. Rowan's mother runs an apothecary shop which ignores modern medicine and still provides remedies like putting a frog in your mouth to cure a cough (the literal "frog in your throat").

Howie is able to identify Rowan's grave. Suspecting foul play of some kind, he wants to exhume the body and bring it back to the mainland to get a full pathology repot. To do so, he will need the permission of the local justice of the peace, Lord Summerisle (Christopher Lee). Summerisle is far more than a local justice; he is in fact the ruler of the island itself. In one of the restored scenes, the viewer has seen Lord Summerisle dressed in Scottish kilts bringing a young teenage boy as an "offering" to the pub owner's very sexual daughter (Britt Ekland). Summerisle says that he is offering the boy to Aphrodite, equating the girl with the ancient goddess. The girl, in apparent modesty at having been addressed as a goddess, responds with the clarification that the offering is "for Aphrodite," thereby taking the role of a priestess of the goddess. Lord Summerisle insists, "I make no such distinction. For him, the girl really is Aphrodite." The scene continues with Summerisle speaking to himself as we see shots of the group in the pub singing their erotic songs along with a shot of Sgt. Howie kneeling beside his bed upstairs in prayer. Lord Summerisle watches two snails making love on a branch and says he is sickened by those whose duty is to God (inset scenes of Howie praying). Summerisle seems to be saying that life is essentially a celebration of fertility, free of any laws or boundaries. For him, this is freedom (insert scenes of the snails copulating). Summerisle adds that none of "them" (the freely erotic following only nature's instincts) are respectable or unhappy.

In some versions of the film, this scene is missing (it is included in the 2014 Final Cut). This scene is important because it gives us clues into Lord Summerisle's character which will become more evident later. At this point, Howie knows nothing of the character of Lord Summerisle. In a critical scene, Howie goes to Summerisle's elegant home to ask permission to exhume Rowan's body. This is the point where Howie is understandably distressed by the scene of young, naked girls leaping over fires. Summerisle, baiting him, asks if the scene of the young people doesn't refresh him. Howie replies curtly, "No, it does not!" Summerisle adds that this is the girls' "divinity lesson." He adds that they are seeking to be impregnated by the gods. Howie virtually explodes at this comment. All he has seen on the island has been, in his mind, sexual depravity reinforced by fake science and fake education. In response to Summerisle's comment about the divinity lesson, Howie asks, "What of the true God whose worship has been celebrated in churches and cathedrals on these islands for generations?" With a slight nod of the head, Summerisle answers, "He's dead. He can't complain. He had his chance and, in modern parlance, blew it." Howie asks, "Have these children never heard of Jesus?" In a muted tone, Summerisle responds that Jesus was born of a virgin impregnated by a ghost, as if to say, Christianity is no different from the ancient religions that it replaced.

As Howie struggles with all this, he is then told the history of Summerisle. It was founded by the present Lord's grandfather, who was a scientist and a free thinker. He developed strains of fruit, especially apples, that could grow on the island because of its unique blend of soil and the warm ocean currents surrounding it. This was the scientific part. He also became a nature worshipper and revived the practice of the "old gods," basically the ancient gods of fertility. As this revival of the ancient gods became established, the churches closed and the ministers left the island. Summerisle adds that his father brought him up the same way, to follow the old gods, to revere nature and to fear it. Howie adds, "He brought you up to be a pagan!" With a slight smile, Summerisle responds, "A heathen perhaps, but hopefully not an unenlightened one."

That night, Howie and a grave digger exhume Rowan Morrison. To his horror, he finds the body of a March Hare. The gravedigger, amused at Howie's shocked response, can only laugh. Howie returns to Summerisle's mansion carrying his grim discovery. He finds Summerisle in his kilts spending the evening with Rowan's attractive teacher (Diane Cilento). He throws the body of the hare before them. Neither one is in the least bit shocked. They act as though the hare really was Rowan's body, now returned to an earlier form of nature. In total frustration, Howie protests that he can't be made a fool of endlessly. The investigation which began with his receipt of an anonymous letter containing a picture of the allegedly missing little girl has gone in circles. With more than a little mockery in his voice, Summerisle comments, "Very perplexing for you." He then adds that Howie is the one who is supposed to be the detective. Howie leaves convinced he has stumbled on to a plot of "pagan barbarity" scarcely imaginable in the twentieth century.

Howie sneaks into the office of records and discovers a photo of the last May Day celebration in which a young girl is surrounded by empty baskets. Howie concludes that the crops had failed the previous year. He then comes to the harrowing conclusion that Rowan must have been kidnapped and hidden, meaning that she will be sacrificed to the ancient gods on May Day to insure the harvest. Howie comments to himself, "Even these people can't be that mad." Yet that seems to be the only possible explanation. He resolves to take his concerns to the mainland the next day.

Howie retires to his bed but Willow, the very erotic daughter of the pub owner, seeks to seduce him. She sings to him and, completely nude, bangs on his wall. She is in the adjacent bedroom, essentially inviting him. In director Robin Hardy and Anthony Shaffer's novelization of the film, Willow stands naked at her doorway in full view of Howie as he goes to his room. Howie's struggle with temptation in that respect is more believable. In the film, he only hears her but never sees her as the viewer does. We also see him get out of bed sweating and struggling against the temptation. He never ventures out of his room.

Howie sleeps in until Willow, now clothed, wakes him. She expresses her disappointment that he did not come to her in the night. He replies that he is engaged to be married. Willow, in her own pagan style, simply asks, why would that stop him? In a remarkable understatement, he adds, "Nothing personal. I just don't believe in it before marriage." We see here the full scope of Howie's character. Despite his rather prudish nature, he is a person of integrity and conviction. Willow adds that, given his convictions, it is probably best that he doesn't stay to see the May Day rituals.

Howie learns that his plans to return to the mainland have been thwarted: The controls of his sea plane have been smashed. No one on the island that will offer him a boat to get back. Howie is convinced that Summerisle and his followers are determined to prevent him from returning to the mainland and sounding an alarm. In an act more of desperation than of good judgment, Howie undertakes his own search for Rowan Morrison. He forces himself into house after house, increasingly becoming a figure of mockery. In one case, he opens the door on the charming Ingrid Pitt taking a bath. Rather than trying to cover herself up, she raises her arm so he can more fully see her breast. Once again Howie has encountered the seductions of the island and, again, he resists.

Led by Lord Summerisle, the island residents gather for the May Day celebration dressed in costumes, many of which are based on animals. Howie has disguised himself as Punch the clown or fool. His plan is to interrupt the sacrifice once it begins. Summerisle sends caskets of ale into the ocean as a libation to the goddess of the sea to go along with their worship of the god of the sun. As everyone is gathered along the coast, Howie sees Rowan in a white dress with flowers in her hair, tied to a rock. He runs to rescue her. She leads him through a tunnel, claiming that this is a way out. Howie sees Lord Summerisle with the schoolteacher, Willow and the seductive woman from the records office (Ingrid Pitt) flanked by all the islanders. The truth begins to dawn on Howie. Rowan is not the sacrificial victim. *He* is. The crops have failed so drastically that even the sacrifice of a child is not adequate. Howie has been studied and tested to make sure that he is the "right kind of sacrifice." The tragedy is that he fits all their requirements. He has come as a representative of the king. He has come alone. He has come dressed as a fool. Finally he has come as a virgin. The irony is that if he had given in to Willow's temptation the previous night, he would have been spared.

Howie shows his true mettle. He believes in the Lord Jesus Christ, the promise of resurrection and the assurance of eternal life. Lord Summerisle comments that in effect they are doing him a favor. He is receiving a rare gift. He will be a martyr and he will be seated with the saints in glory.

In spite of his strong faith, Howie is also a realist. He doesn't want to die, not like this anyway. He confronts the crowd with the fact that they are about to commit murder. His death will not bring back their fruit. The artificial strain they had introduced into the soil could not last. It was against the nature of the island. In a highly charged moment, Howie adds that since he knows their sacrifice will be futile, their only choice the coming year will be to sacrifice no one less than Lord Summerisle himself. In stern language, Lord Summerisle states that the sacrifice of the king-fool-virgin will be accepted. It will not fail. Yet his tone suggests that he is saying this to convince himself more than anything else.

Howie is prepared for the sacrifice. While held by a strong islander named Oak, his clothes are removed and replaced by a white gown. The three erotic women he has encountered on the island pour water on him and brush him with their hair. Summerisle intones, "It is time to keep your appointment with the Wicker Man." The Wicker Man turns out to be just that, a giant man-like figure made out of wicker. In the compartments of the figure are animals, presumably part of the sacrifice. Howie screams at the sight of it. Oak carries him up a ladder and he is imprisoned in a top area of the figure. In spite of his fear, Howie retains his composure. He prays to his God. At one point he partially quotes from the Book of Joel in the Old Testament (Howie really knows his scripture):

> Be ye ashamed, O ye husbandmen; howl, O ye vinedressers, for the wheat and for the barley; because the harvest of the field is perished. The vine is dried up, and the fig tree languisheth; the pomegranate tree, the palm tree also and the apple tree, even all the trees of the field, are withered; because joy is withered away from the sons of men. (Joel 1:11–12).

In ominous tones, Lord Summerisle, his hair blowing in the wind, says, "Reverence the sacrifice." Torches light the giant wicker figure and it starts to burn. Howie starts singing the 23rd psalm that we heard him sing in the church service at the start of the film. In contrast, Summerisle leads the crowd singing "Summer is a-comin' in." They sway to and fro as they sing. Director Robin Hard said in interviews that his model for this was documentaries of Nazi political rallies.

The giant Wicker Man, fully aflame, collapses. We hear the screeching of geese and Howie's final cry calling out to Jesus. The camera then pans toward the setting sun. We hear the sounds of trumpets. The novel states, in the words of John Bunyan's *The Pilgrim's Progress,* that these trumpets were sounding for Howie as he comes to the "other side." He is an example of Bunyan's character, Valiant-for-Truth.

The film is open to many interpretation. Howie is no great scholar or leader like Van Helsing or the Duc de Richleau. His strict, somewhat limited Christian faith makes him even more believable. At times he sounds archaic with this confidence that Scotland still is a Christian nation, a dubious claim even in 1973. Lord Summerisle at times sounds like a post-modern liberal. Yet in the moment of the sacrifice, our sympathies are naturally with Howie rather than the pagan inhabitants of the island.

Christopher Lee as Lord Summerisle

There several major aspects to Lee's performance of Lord Summerisle. These no doubt derive in large part from how the character is written in

Anthony Shaffer's screenplay. Nonetheless, Lee's performance both expands and interprets the role.

Our first view of him is in the role of a pagan high priest. He comes by night offering a young boy to Willow, whom he calls "Aphrodite." In this early scene, we are presented with the theme of human sacrifice, which is central to the film. Summerisle is the one making the sacrifice. Not only is the boy being initiated into sexual activity, but this is also a religious rite which foreshadows other religious rites in the film, leading up to the final burnt human sacrifice. Summerisle clearly relishes his role.

However, his monologue about how he is sickened by those who dutifully serve their God (read: Sgt. Howie), adding that those who follow the direct impulses of nature are neither respectable nor unhappy, is something different. Lee is able to introduce into the character an important element which will exist in tension in Summerisle's character throughout the film. Contrary to his own statements, Summerisle is not a pure pagan. His paganism throughout is referenced to his rejection of Christianity. His belief is not simply the revival or indeed continuation of fertility worship and nature gods. It is in reality an expression of his negative reaction to those who serve their God as a duty and are "respectable."

Rather than being a pure pagan, Summerisle is essentially an apostate. His denial of Christianity implies that at some level he was a believer. Ostensibly he was raised as a "heathen." Yet he knows the content of the Christian faith in detail, to the point where he can describe Howie's death as martyrdom, as the early Christians were sacrificed to the ancient gods of Rome. A pure pagan would celebrate the rites of Aphrodite or whomever as an end in itself. They would not need to somehow justify their action. Summerisle's comment in his opening scene indicates that he is struggling with a tension between the role of pagan priest and post–Christian apostate.

Summerisle's first encounter with Sgt. Howie bears this out. Following his explanation of his somewhat scientific paganism which provided for the growth of fruit on the island, Howie asks him, "What of the true God?" It's striking how Summerisle answers. He doesn't deny the existence of the Christian God. He simply says, "Oh, he's dead. He can't complain. He had his chance." This is not pure denial. It is rather the acknowledgment of something that once existed but is no more. Shaffer no doubt put this in the script but it's the way that Lee delivers the line that gives it multiple shadings. Summerisle does not say this in some triumphant fashion. Rather he states his view in muted, almost hesitant tones. It suggests that Summerisle had some experience of faith which he now seeks to reject. To say that something has died is also to say that it was once alive.

The continuing tension between Summerisle's role as pagan priest and apostate Christian is at the core of Lee's performance. When Howie mentions Jesus, Summerisle responds by, in effect, describing Jesus in terms of classic myth. He states that Jesus was born of a virgin who was impregnated by a "ghost." Referencing that simple statement is really to say that Jesus is no different than Greek heroes such as Hercules who had mortal mothers and divine fathers. But Summerisle omits elements that he would have to have known. Whatever one thinks of the Christian concept of the Virgin Birth, there are two very distinctive differences that it has when compared to classic myths. First, Jesus' birth is in a definite historical context. Jesus is born into a setting with real historical figures such as Caesar Augustus and Herod the Great. Second, Jesus' conception is presented in asexual terms. There is no physical, sexual act that leads to Jesus' birth. To the contrary, Mary remains a virgin while the Holy Spirit comes upon her (Luke 1:35). Greek myths presented strange and even ingenious forms of conception such as Zeus impregnating Perseus' mother Danae by coming upon her in a shower of gold. This certainly is highly unusual but it still represents a physical encounter.

One part of Summerisle's character is that he is an enlightened modern, even post-modern figure. We see him as a gracious host during Howie's first visit to his home. He represents a dual approach to nature. On one side, as he tells Howie about his grandfather, he is scientific. On the other, he reveres the old gods and fears them. In reality he sees the two as joined together. Nature is both impersonal following scientific laws and also personal in the form of the gods of the sun and the sea. He mentions the fact that these "reforms" on the island led to the closing of the churches and the departure of the ministers. Later, the schoolteacher mentions that the island's cemetery can no longer be called a churchyard since Christianity has been abandoned.

On the surface, Howie and Summerisle would appear to be polar opposites in terms of their beliefs. Yet there are parallels between them. Howie holds onto his faith at all costs. It's severely tested by Willow's attempted seduction of him. His ultimate test comes when he is facing his sacrificial death. Even then, his faith remains. Summerisle's faith is also tested. His rejection of Christianity is as foundational to his beliefs as Howie's acceptance of Christ is to him. Yet as the film intensifies, Summerisle's rejection of Christianity and his acceptance of the old gods is not as firm as he would have others believe. In the climax when Howie becomes painfully aware that he is "the right kind of adult" for the sacrifice, we have a final confrontation between Howie and Summerisle.

In their first two encounters, Summerisle seems to have the upper hand. His description of his frank paganism leads to Howie's verdict that Summerisle is a pagan. Summerisle makes the intriguing remark, "A heathen perhaps, but hopefully not an unenlightened one." What does he mean by this? On one level, it can refer to his scientific and historical consciousness of the work of his grandfather and father. It can certainly also refer to his knowledge of Howie's faith. However, as we have suggested, that knowledge seems to be selective, not because of any ignorance on his part but rather as an attempt to avoid issues that might challenge his dismissal of this God whom he claims is dead.

In the second encounter, Summerisle has even more of an upper hand. Howie is both shocked and confused at having found a dead March Hare in what was supposedly Rowan Morrison's grave. Summerisle and his woman companion seem to adopt the view that the hare is somehow Rowan's transmuted form. In response to Howie's bewilderment, Summerisle none too subtly reminds Howie that he is supposed to be the detective.

The third encounter is very different. Initially it appears again that Summerisle has the advantage. Howie has been duped into thinking that Rowan will be the sacrifice when in fact he will be the victim. Faced with something that he can barely imagine, Howie turns to his faith. In a loud voice he asserts his belief in Christ and the hope of the resurrection. Summerisle comments on this faith, showing that he understands exactly what Howie is talking about. Howie then challenges Summerisle on scientific grounds. The island could not sustain the growth planned by his grandfather. Howie presses the point that his death will not benefit the crops and that next year, *Summerisle* will have to be the sacrifice. Summerisle professes his conviction that "they will not fail." Yet the expression on his face and the tone of his voice not only shows that he is trying to convince himself but, at a deeper level, he knows that what Howie predicts will in fact come true. The real truth is that Summerisle is not fully convinced of his own paganism. His faith is a desperate one. His response here has been building up throughout he entire film beginning with his reflection on his earlier offering of a young boy to "Aphrodite," on up to his comment about the death of God. In all this we see, now especially, that he is not fully convinced of his own creed. There is doubt at the very heart of it. His response to Howie's prediction of his death elicits a statement of confidence in the present sacrifice ("It will not fail"). Yet his tone and look goes beyond self-doubt. Lee communicates an air of resignation. It is as if he accepts the fundamental fatalism of Greek mythology (Oedipus will murder his father and marry his mother no matter what he does to seek to avoid that fate). Finally, what Lee suggests is that, in his core, he knows that what Howie says is the truth. In this respect, as we have noted, he is more post–Christian than non–Christian. When he calls for the commencement of the sacrifice, he is also grim-faced. At the end as the Wicker Man burns, he attempts a joyful, celebratory look. Yet that is at variance with what we have just seen.

The film is framed by Summerisle's response to the two sacrifices, the first a young boy to a goddess, the second the burning of Howie. In terms of the pagan beliefs which he claim to espouse, both sacrifices are warranted. They both deal with fertility and the cycle of life. The greatest fear that ancient peoples had was the fear of famine. While wars and plagues could be devastating, famine wiped out everyone. The cycle of life requires both life and death. More specifically, for something to live, something else must die. Therefore the two "sacrifices" are bookends to each other. The encounter with Aphrodite is a statement of life. The burnt offering is a statement of death. Both are necessary within the belief system that Summerisle claims to espouse. Yet in both instances we have seen that Summerisle has somehow to convince himself of all this.

Howie's belief is simple and uncomplicated. His faith has its own tensions. The celebration of Holy Communion also deals with death and life. Yet this is a one-time sacrifice which takes away all sin with the promise of eternal life (Hebrews 9:11–15). Summerisle's belief requires ongoing, continuing sacrifices. At best it can only offer life for a year at a time and needs to be repeated simply to maintain temporal life. Summerisle in his reflections and responses manifests a fundamental doubt in what he claims to believe. Lee's expression suggests that these doubts intensify the more he directly sees the essence of Howie's faith. In the final analysis, Howie's death is triumphant whereas Summerisle's faith can only guarantee him one more year. His tone and demeanor communicate this.

One of the great strengths of Lee's performance (as well as that of the film as a whole) is its sense of ambiguity. Part of this is communicated by the storyline of the film. For all its accolades as a horror film, the picture functions like a mystery. A child is missing—but no one, including the child's presumed mother, admits her existence. Lee certainly communicates this same ambiguity in his portrayal. The film in fact has multiple ambiguities. Many questions are left unanswered. For example, was this the only time that crops had failed more than one year in succession? If there had been other times like this, how was the sacrifice located and enticed to the island? Summerisle at the climax speaks of the painstaking research that had been done on Howie. How was this "research" carried out? How was it done without arousing suspicion? This is especially questionable given the fact that the island dwellers and Lord Summerisle himself, seem fully contained in their island culture. Howie makes the obvious point that he will be missed, that others will come looking for him. He is, after all, a police sergeant. Summerisle simply states that they will find no trace. It is a credit to the director and to Lee's performance that the film hurries on without giving the viewer much time to consider that this is an obvious weakness in the islanders' plot.

Presumably the plan will be to destroy Howie's boat plane. His clothes and any other personal belongings will also have to disappear. More to the point, what about Rowan? In a scene missing from the so-called Final Cut, Howie discusses the letter he has received claiming that Rowan is missing with his police station colleagues. More than that, someone as meticulous as Howie would presumably leave a record of where he was going and why. Anyone investigating his disappearance would also want to know what happened to the missing girl. Will Rowan have to remain in hiding until that investigation is complete? The islanders themselves will have to be trusted to hide the truth. Granted, they did that when Howie first arrived. However, his first clue was the fact that Rowan's sister revealed her identity. What about the children who, along with Rowan, witness the sacrifice? Couldn't one of them break down under questioning? The investigation of a missing police officer will not be satisfied with cursory answers.

There are other potential flaws in the scheme. What if Howie had given in to the temptation of the nude Willow calling to him from the next room? In this regard, the film is more believable than the subsequent novel in that in the film Howie never actually sees the naked "goddess," which lends more credibility to his resistance. Yet suppose he had given in? That would have disqualified him as "the right kind of adult." Did Summerisle have a plan B? Supposedly they would have to have let Howie go. Presumably, knowing he had capitulated in the night, there would have been no need to sabotage his boat plane. However, Howie's plan in that case would be to return to the mainland to get reinforcements and return to solve the case of the missing Rowan. In that case, any number of questions would be posed that would be very difficult for Summerisle and the other islanders to answer.

It is a credit to both the direction and screenplay that we are not bothered by these incongruities. While they are touched on, we remain so absorbed in the central action that they don't really intrude on us until long after we've viewed the film and experienced its impact. Credit has to be given also to the cast that keeps us off guard. The greatest credit however has to be given to Christopher Lee. Lee's character is at the core ambiguities of the film. They are in fact in the essence of his character. Yet Lee's multi-dimensional performance keeps us glued to the events on screen. We don't worry about the loose plot threads. Lee draws us in with a fascinating performance which holds our attention throughout.

The ambiguities go beyond these direct plot issues. Given the constant, almost indiscriminate lovemaking on the island (beginning with teenage boys who are given as "offerings"), one would expect a rash of unplanned pregnancies, to say nothing of sexually transmitted diseases. Add to this the fact that modern medicine seems to be in short supply given the strange treatments offered even for a sore throat. What about disease in general and indeed any form of medical treatment? We are told that there are no ministers on the island. What about doctors? And, if there were, what would they think about the odd cures being offered?

The conflict between good and evil which surfaces here is also ambiguous. It is not easily recognized in the course of the film. We can be put off by Howie's authoritarian and rigid manner. Humility is not his greatest strength. On the other hand, Lee presents Summerisle as gracious and even appealing. He is essentially an attractive figure. Yet in the tradition of the best horror films, the source of evil is deceptive. Satan indeed can masquerade as an angel of light. The British director of most of the classic Hammer films, Terence Fisher, once said in an interview that if evil were ugly, it wouldn't be a problem. As *The Wicker Man* unfolds, we find ourselves confronted with the reality of human sacrifice (which apparently had been a child sacrifice the previous year). However, the tragedy is that Howie doesn't suspect what is really happening until it is too late.

This is often the case in dealing with the reality of evil. Lee in this performance, along with many others, shows us the attraction of evil. The implication is clear. We need to recognize the darkness before it overcomes us.

10

I Monster (1971)

I Monster is yet another version of the Robert Louis Stevenson novella *The Strange Case of Dr. Jekyll and Mr. Hyde.* Produced by Amicus, a chief rival to Hammer in British horror films of the 1960s and '70s, it stars Christopher Lee as Jekyll and Hyde. The names in this case have been changed to Dr. Marlowe and Mr. Blake (was there an intentional choice of famous surnames of British authors?). In spite of this unexplained difference, the film as a whole is one of the closest ever produced to Stevenson's original. Interestingly, the other characters in the story all have the names that Stevenson gave them originally. It is no wonder that this story is one of the most filmed in history (there were at least five versions in the silent era alone). Its continuing fascination lies in the fact that it is one of the best examples in all of literature of the essential conflict between good and evil.

This was not the first time that Lee had appeared in a screen version of this classic story: Lee appeared in Hammer's startling *The Two Faces of Dr. Jekyll* (*House of Fright* in the U.S.), in which Canadian actor Paul Massie appeared as a bearded Dr. Jekyll who changed into a clean-shaven and very attractive Mr. Hyde. Directed Terence Fisher applied his concept of the beauty of evil to the story. Two years after *I Monster,* Hammer did another innovative version, *Dr. Jekyll and Sister Hyde,* in which Hyde is a beautiful woman. There were also comic versions of the story done at this time including Hammer's *The Ugly Duckling* (1959) and Jerry Lewis' *The Nutty Professor* (1963). In the midst of these various reinterpretations, Amicus' version followed the Stevenson original fairly closely.

In Victorian London, Dr. Marlowe (Lee) enters a club where he finds three of his friends: his lawyer Mr. Utterson (Peter Cushing), Mr. Enfield (Mike Raven) and Dr. Lanyon (Richard Hurndall). Talking about the recent hanging of a notorious criminal leads to a discussion of good and evil in human beings. Enfield expresses the view that some people, like the condemned criminal, are inherently evil while Dr. Lanyon believes that people are fundamentally good, and that society or circumstance can turn them to evil. Marlowe's view is that human beings are a mixture of good and evil. He ties this in with the recent work of Dr. Sigmund Freud in Vienna. Civilization forces us to resist our desires and impulses. Utterson states that such resistance to our wants and wishes are essential for the common good of society.

Marlowe has done more than simply think about the division in human beings. What's added to the story here is his effort to relate it to Freud's early work. Marlowe psychoanalyzes his patients. This comes into play as Marlowe becomes more intrigued with Freud's idea of repression, which appears to hold one side of humanity's two-sided nature at bay. Marlowe has developed a drug which he believes can separate the two natures. He holds to the basic view that if the repressed side of each person could be openly expressed, human beings would be more healthy and productive.

This reasoning is close to what we have in other versions of the story. Stevenson's own account of Jekyll's experiments is Jekyll's belief that if the lower part of human nature could have its moment of indulgence, it would free the higher side of human nature to achieve greater goals. Marlowe has developed a drug which can accomplish this purpose. Instead of being a potion which he drinks (as in in the book and in other film versions), Mar-

Christopher Lee as the Dr. Jekyll counterpart in *I Monster* (1971).

lowe's drug would be injected into his arm. This image of an injection in 1971 played into the drug culture of the period.

Marlowe, about to experiment on himself, hesitates, then decides to inject the drug into a cat. It becomes ferocious and wildly attacks him. Without fully realizing what he is doing, Marlowe beats the cat to death. Next his butler, Poole (George Merritt), informs him that one of his patients is anxious to see him. "At this hour?" Marlowe asks. Poole responds that the woman is most insistent.

The woman is deeply troubled. He has been treating her using the psychoanalytic method he learned from Freud, but she has made little progress. Marlowe asks her if she would be willing to try something experimental; the anxious woman is open to anything. He injects her with his drug and leaves her in the consulting room for a few minutes. When he returns, he finds that she has disrobed and is now trying to seduce him. He resists her, then injects her with the drug again. The woman reverts back to her former self, now ashamed of her conduct.

Marlowe tries the drug on another patient, a burly, domineering man. It makes him timid and weepy. Now at last, Marlowe tries the drug on himself. It initially gives him a sense of euphoria.

Marlowe now begins a double life, as himself and his alter ego Edward Blake (Hyde). Blake initially does not have the appearance of a monster, just a sinister-looking version of Marlowe. As he continues to use the drug, his appearance becomes distorted and ugly. Marlowe interprets what is happening in Freudian terms: The issue is not good and evil but repression and conscious behavior. The drug brings out the hidden side of the person. Hence, a shy, anxious woman becomes bold and assertive. The drug has the opposite effect on a domineering man. At one point, Marlowe discusses his views with his mentor, Dr. Lanyon, without revealing the full extent of his experiments. They discuss the classic distinctions of Freud's theory. There is the id which expresses the primitive and basic drives of the person. This is followed by the ego, which is the conscious self, and finally the super-ego which represents the whole area of morality and social restraint. Marlowe talks about freeing the id (the part that is usually suppressed) so that it can satisfy its desires without the restraint of the super-ego. Lanyon cautions that a person acting apart from both the restraint and the guidance of the super-ego would be a danger to himself and society. He would in effect be a monster. Lanyon still holds to the view that human beings are essentially good. This goodness would seem to come from both the ego's conscious desires and the super-ego's restraints, which hold the desires of the id in check. What is noteworthy is that what began at the start of the film as a discussion of good and evil has become a psychological issue.

In Stevenson's original story there is no mention of Freud, though certainly there are implications of his theories in the whole account of Jekyll's two sides. In the novella, Jekyll is a middle-aged man while Hyde appears much younger and indeed more energetic. In this sense, Hyde is underdeveloped. Jekyll has suppressed that side of his nature which, of course, is another name for repression. This whole discussion between Marlowe and Lanyon does not occur in the book though again one could argue that something like it would seem to be implied.

The film next presents us with important scenes in the book which are largely absent from other film versions. The first (and the most disturbing) involves a little girl. Enfield and Utterson are walking along a street when Enfield tells a remarkable story of an event that occurred one night when he was on that same street: He saw a little girl run into a man in a top hat and cape. The man pushed her down onto the street and then trampled her! Hearing the little girl's cries, people ran to the scene. Enfield himself went after the man, who was trying to walk away. The people insisted that the man make a payment to the girl's parents. The man went into a ramshackle apart-

Christopher Lee as the Mr. Hyde counterpart in *I Monster* (1971).

ment house and emerged with a check. What shocked Enfield was that the check was signed by Marlowe. In the morning, the check was taken to the bank where it was determined that the signature was genuine. This shocking incident is shown in this version; to my knowledge, the only other time is in the 1920 John Barrymore version (where the victim is a little boy). At this point, we only hear of the incident; later we see it in flashback.

Utterson is shaken by all this but he has his own story to tell as Marlowe's attorney. Marlowe has made a new will specifying that in the event of his death or his unexplained disappearance, his home and all his wealth and possessions are to be given over to Edward Blake. Utterson also learns that the servants have been instructed to allow Blake full run of the house and are to comply with all his requests. Blake has a key to the outside door of the laboratory. Utterson is convinced that Marlowe is being blackmailed by Blake. We, the viewers, of course, know different.

Determined to meet Blake face to face, Utterson waits near the laboratory doorway. Eventually Blake appears and as he is about to unlock the door Utterson taps him on the shoulder. Marlowe pushes him away and disappears into the house. Utterson notes that Blake carries a distinctive and elegant cane which in fact he stole one night by breaking the window of a shop and stealing it.

As Marlowe continues his double life, Blake becomes uglier and more menacing. Blake goes to a tavern and tries to entice a woman (Marjie Lawrence). She starts to accompany him, no doubt thinking that he is rich in spite of his facial appearance. One of the denizens of the tavern demands to know why he is leaving with her. At this point, she backs away saying, "Do you think I was leaving with *him*!?" Everyone begins to laugh at him. The humiliated Blake leaves, barely concealing his rage. He waits outside until the woman leaves. Blake begins stalking her. Realizing that he is after her, she runs. Finally he corners her in an alleyway. Thinking that he wants to rape her, she is prepared to give in. "All right, then, come on!" she says as she begins to lift up her skirt. Blake is not interested in sex. He attacks her with his cane, killing her. The top half of the cane breaks off in the attack and Blake leaves it behind. In the original story, an unprovoked Hyde murders Sir Danvers Carew, whom he beats to death with his cane which also breaks in the attack and becomes a critical clue to the identity of the murderer.

Marlowe resolves to have nothing more to do with Blake. He tells Utterson that he has broken off with Blake and shows him a letter which he claims that Blake had sent him, saying he was leaving the country for good. Marlowe talks about the ugliness of evil, which becomes worse the more one sees it.

The savage murder of the woman is under investigation. Utterson sees a picture of the cane in the newspaper and recognizes it as Blake's. He is convinced that Blake was intending to murder Marlowe. He tells Marlowe, "You have had a narrow escape." His interpretation is logical but, of course, wrong.

Marlowe walks in the park as a Salvation Army band plays the hymn "Jesus Shall Reign." This isone of several religious references in the film: In the apartment building where Blake takes a room, there is a framed picture with the inscription, "In the hand of God." At another point, we see a picture of a woman praying.

A little boy is playing with a ball in the park where Marlowe is sitting. This conjures up the image of the little girl he trampled. All of a sudden, Marlowe begins to change into Blake. He rushes off, frightening everyone including the band players. Blake now is wanted for the murder of the girl. In renouncing his identity as Blake, Marlowe had put away all the keys, including the street entrance to the laboratory. The servants have been advised to call the police immediately if Blake returns. Blake needs to get his drug without being caught. This is one of the most suspenseful parts of Stevenson's original story and it recurs in virtually every dramatization of *Jekyll and Hyde.*

Blake sends a note (signed Marlowe) to Dr. Lanyon asking him, for the sake of their old friendship, to go to his laboratory and get the drug. Lanyon finds the drug and brings it to his home. Shortly thereafter, Blake appears, claiming to be acting on Marlowe's behalf. Lanyon refuses to let him leave until he has revealed Marlowe's whereabouts and indeed can vouch for his safety. Blake relents with the ominous warning, "Let this be on your head." Blake injects himself with the drug and turns back into Marlowe before Lanyon's horrified eyes. Marlowe leaves as Lanyon succumbs to a fatal heart attack as a result of what he has seen.

Utterson's suspicions are growing. He learns from Poole that no messenger delivered Blake's final letter. He compares Blake's letter with one that he had received from Marlowe. The two are identical. It must be said here that the role of Utterson, which is virtually missing from most other film adaptations, picks up a key character from the original story. Stevenson's original work is structured like a mystery with Utterson being in effect the detective. He plays the same role in this film. However, in the book, Utterson and the servants break down the locked laboratory door only to find the dead body of Hyde. Utterson is then able to piece together the truth from written statements of both Dr. Lanyon and Dr. Jekyll.

In this version, as Marlowe is no longer able to keep from turning into Blake even without the drug, Blake becomes convinced (quite rightly) that Utterson is getting close to the truth. Blake goes to Utterson's home with the intention of murdering him. A fight ensues and a fire breaks out with Blake finally falling to his death down Utterson's stairs. In death, Blake turns back into Marlowe, and now Utterson knows the whole truth.

To begin to evaluate the film, we have to see it in the larger context of film history, including the extensive role that the story of *The Strange Case of Dr. Jekyll and Mr. Hyde* plays in that history.

Dr. Jekyll and Mr. Hyde: *The Original Story*

Stevenson's original story was more than a little shocking when it first appeared in 1886. This was prior to the appearance of Sherlock Holmes and Dracula. While ghost stories were popular in Victorian England, the Gothic novel with its often graphic monsters and madmen had largely dropped out of popularity following satires like Jane Austin's *Northanger Abbey.* That was published the same year (1818) as Mary Shelley's *Frankenstein,* which in many ways represented the culmination of the whole Gothic tradition. Edgar Allan Poe carried on but only in short stories, as did the Irish writer J. Sheridan LeFanu, whose novella *Carmilla* was an influence on *Dracula.*

This is to say that *Dr. Jekyll and Mr. Hyde* was in many ways a striking departure from what many regarded the norm in literature (so-called "penny dreadfuls" were considered outside the purview of literature). Stevenson doesn't elaborate but when he referred to Hyde's activities as "drinking pleasure with bestial avidity from any degree of torture to another," many Victorian readers were more than taken aback. Stevenson's work really operates on three fundamental levels, and each deals with the theme of good vs. evil. On an initial level, the story is a religious allegory. Stevenson was raised in a strict Scottish Presbyterian home. While he broke away from the church in his adult years, what he learned in his youth were still with him. The strict Calvinism of the Church of Scotland taught that human beings were "totally depraved." It must be qualified that, theologically, this didn't mean that people were as depraved as they could possibly be. It did mean that every aspect of human life was tainted by sin. This sin had to be resisted for the sake of each person's soul but this was not thought to be humanly possible. Only God's grace, freely given in Jesus Christ, wiped away the effects of sin. Yet even in the believer, the power of sin still remained.

The concept of good and evil warring within the soul of even the most devout Christian was a basic New Testament teaching. In the seventh chapter of the Letter to the Romans, Paul writes,

For I know that nothing good dwells within me, that is, in my flesh. I can will what is right, but I cannot do it. For I do not do the good I want, but the evil I do not want is what I do. Now if I do what I do not want it is no longer I that do it, but sin that dwells within me. So I find it to be a law that when I want to do what is good, evil lies close at hand (Romans 7:18–21).

This duality lies at the heart of Stevenson's classic tale. Jekyll's cardinal mistake lies in his thinking that the good in him is stronger than the evil. He thinks that the evil side, once satisfied, will not impair the good, which can then rise to greater heights. The view that is described here was one which was common to many mid–Victorians. This is the second level of Stevenson's story. Charles Darwin's *The Origin of Species* had been published in 1859. The theory of evolution in a popular form was meant to describe an inevitable progress of human beings and their world. There was an essential confidence in the basic goodness of human beings. The obstacles to the full realization of this goodness came from either ignorance or negative social conditions like poverty or unjust laws that imprisoned people for not paying their debts. The essential problem of human existence was not internal but external.

Stevenson's story, which electrified the nation, challenged all that. Jekyll suffered the consequences of a naïve view that evil did not come from within the human heart but was an external, largely social problem. As such, it could eventually be eliminated through a combination of education and good social planning. Darwin's view of evolution underlined all this with its popular interpretation of inevitable progress (a view which tended to ignore Darwin's own descriptions of the inherent struggles of the evolutionary process). Priests and ministers seized on the example of Jekyll and Hyde in numerous sermons as a way of re-emphasizing the ancient doctrine of sin.

There was a third level to Stevenson's masterpiece. In 1872, German philosopher Friedrich Nietzsche published his first book, *The Birth of Tragedy*, and introduced another interpretation of the duality of human nature based on Greek mythology. He argued that an emotionally healthy person needed to be a combination of the traits of Apollo and Dionysius, both sons of Zeus. In Nietzsche's interpretation, Apollo represented rationality, logic and responsibility. Dionysus, the god of wine, signified irrationality, myth and indulgence. Nietzsche's argument was that we have to do honor to both gods. Yes, of course we need to be rational and responsible, otherwise civilization would not be possible. At the same time, however, there is an essential life source in Dionysus. There is an irrational, emotional side of life which has to be acknowledged and experienced.

Stevenson's duality of Jekyll and Hyde at one level could be traced to Nietzsche's dichotomy of Apollo-Dionysus. But Stevenson's view of this duality was radically different from Nietzsche's. Obviously Jekyll represented the Apollo side and Hyde the Dionysian. Jekyll sincerely believes that he can combine both and even enhance his life thereby. He is of course wrong. Once Hyde is indulged, he inevitably will take over the whole personality. Worse, by indulging his bestial desires he will descend to the point where he becomes pure evil. In Greek myth, Dionysus takes horrible revenge on all those who oppose his indulgent practices. He drives them into madness where they even eat their own children. Stevenson, in effect, is saying that giving in to the Dionysian side even once can lead to destruction.

The impact of Stevenson's work led quickly to efforts to dramatize the story. A theatrical version made its appearance two years after its publication. Jekyll was given a fiancée to add depth to the story. The power of the production can be seen in the fact that in the wake of the Jack the Ripper murders, the play was cancelled. The advent of film brought more possibilities not only to dramatize elements like Jekyll's transformation into Hyde but also to visualize what Stevenson had called Hyde's "bestial avidity."

Jekyll and Hyde—the Film Versions

Prior to the filming of *I Monster,* there had been at least a dozen earlier film versions, not to mention sequels like *Daughter of Dr. Jekyll* and comic versions like *Abbott and Costello Meet Dr. Jekyll and Mr. Hyde.* The first film version appeared in 1908. There were at least eight versions in the silent era, the most notable being Paramount's 1920 version which starred John Barrymore. Barrymore at the time was emerging as one of America's greatest actors.

In this version, Jekyll, an idealistic doctor, runs a charity hospital for poor people. He is engaged to Millicent Carew, the daughter of the well-to-do Sir George Carew. At a dinner party, Sir George mocks Jekyll's goodness and challenges Jekyll to explore other sides of life. He makes the comment, "If I use my right hand should I not also lose my left?" suggesting a kind of ying-yang view.

Carew entices Jekyll to a night club in London where he encounters a seductive dancer, Miss Gina. Intrigued, Jekyll begins to explore this neglected side of himself which, of course, after taking the drug, emerges as Mr. Hyde. Hyde almost forcibly takes Miss Gina. After exploiting and abusing her, he goes after another woman in a tavern. Gina, now disheveled, is also present. In a bizarre moment, he drags the two women before a mirror to (in effect) show a "before and after."

The issue in this version is not suppression but simply lack of exposure.

What is unique here is that Jekyll's future father-in-law functions as a tempter, leading Jekyll into evil. Just before Hyde kills Carew, he confronts him with the fact that Carew is basically to blame for his degeneration into Hyde since Carew first tempted him. This somewhat weakens the story since Jekyll is not struggling internally, morally or emotionally, but rather succumbs all too easily the influence of Carew. Nonetheless, Barrymore's spider-like Hyde is a very formidable creation.

In 1931, Paramount produced a talkie version directed by the innovative Rouben Mamoulian. It makes striking use of subjective camera, split scenes and unusual dissolves. The transformation scene employing a series of sounds and whirling camera shots remains effective to this day. Many regard this version as the best film treatment of the story.

But the film never really comes together in its view of the relationship of Jekyll to Hyde. Jekyll in an early sequence gives a speech insisting that man is "not one but two." But we are never completely told what those "two" are. For Stevenson they are of course good and evil. The view in this film seems to be that on one side, there is an essentially Freudian dualism between the repressed self, due to social convention, and the public self which follows those social conventions. Jekyll here evidences repressed sexuality both with regard to his fiancée Muriel and a pub singer named Ivy. But the depiction of Hyde seems also to draw on an evolutionary model since Hyde here clearly has apelike qualities.

The film has many notable qualities not the least of which is Mamoulian's florid direction. Yet in the final analysis, the relationship of Jekyll and Hyde remains unclear. We go from Freudian repression to evolutionary change to the final issue of good vs. evil in very Christian terms with Jekyll desperately (but ineffectively) trying to pray. Even so, the prevailing impression is of Hyde as a kind of ape man. It is one thing to discuss Freud's view as an interpretation (which effectively occurs in *I Monster*) and another simply to insert his view on repression into the narrative. In spite of the overall excellence of the film with its strong atmosphere of Victorian London, expressionist touches and an Oscar-winning performance by Fredric March as Jekyll and Hyde, we are left with a confused view of the dualism that is at the heart of the story.

A similar problem occurs in the next major film version, MGM's 1941 remake. This film too often has been dismissed as inferior to the Mamoulian version. This is not really fair since, even though it follows the same narrative outline, it has a different emphasis. Its outstanding cast includes Spencer Tracy as Jekyll and Hyde, Lana Turner as his fiancée and Ingrid Bergman as Ivy, the barmaid tormented by Hyde. The difficulty in this version is that the two natures of Jekyll and Hyde are not delineated clearly enough. The film introduces Jekyll with his fiancée and future father-in-law in a church service in which a disturbed man, Higgins, has an outburst and has to be taken away to a hospital. Jekyll hopes to try out his theory of the two personalities in human beings by giving Higgins his drug. Jekyll believes that a work-related accident caused Higgins' "evil" side to emerge and take over his whole personality. When asked to explain his view, Jekyll uses the terms good and evil, but seems really to be defining normal behavior over against abnormal. Higgins is described as being normally good until an accident shocked his system and brought out not so much evil as abnormal behavior (interrupting a church service).

Jekyll plans to experiment on Higgins but a hospital supervisor strongly objects. Jekyll would be treating a human being as little more than a lab rat. Jekyll feels that science cannot be limited to what he calls hidebound morality. He claims that advances in science have to go beyond established norms. This is a very different Jekyll than the figure in both the Barrymore and March versions, who spent most of their spare time caring for the poor in charity hospitals.

When his drug is prepared, he goes to the hospital intending to try it out on Higgins. When he learns that Higgins has just died, Jekyll decides to try it on himself. Up to this point he has attempted it only on animals, with the result that the animals became the opposite of their normal selves. A rat becomes docile while a rabbit turns vicious. Jekyll takes the drug and proceeds to have a wild dream where he, as Jekyll, is whipping two horses which change into the two women in his life. We see only the women's heads and bare shoulders, so they appear to be nude. This scene with its Freudian and surrealistic overtones has sometimes been dismissed as excessive or just plain silly. Yet it's a remarkable sequence, especially for MGM and the strict Production Code of the period. When we finally see Hyde after the transformation, his resemblance to Jekyll is notable. When Ivy goes to Jekyll for help, she sees the similarity. Hyde later taunts her as he is about to kill her, confronting her with the fact that she saw something of Hyde in Jekyll.

Here is the fundamental problem with this version: Jekyll and Hyde are too similar. The early scenes of Jekyll's desiring to experiment on a deranged man and his sadistic dream of whipping the two women establish him as an abusive figure. In spite of his mild-mannered character in much of the rest of the film, these early scenes reveal his own deranged character. Changing into Hyde merely brings this to its full realization. Stevenson's original conflict between good and evil along with his focus on the evil tendency in every person is de-emphasized here in favor of a variation on the repressed personality theme. Whereas Fredric March's portrayal focused on the repression of a normal sexual drive, Tracy's presents a tendency for abuse from the very beginning. We are left with the question, is Tracy's Jekyll no less disturbed than Higgins? The net effect of these classic Hollywood versions is that the primary focus of Stevenson's story is played down in favor of a psychological interpretation. Those elements are present in the original novel but the focus there is on the warring conflict between good and evil in the human soul. In each of these classic films, that central theme is watered down.

There is one other major film adaptation that has already been mentioned, Hammer Films' 1960 adaptation with the intriguing title *The Two Faces of Dr. Jekyll.* Christopher Lee appears in this film though not in the title role. This is a fairly loose adaptation. Its most notable feature is the fact that Hyde, instead of being ugly and frightening, is handsome and charming—a touch of Dorian Gray in other words. Lee plays Paul, a friend of Jekyll. Jekyll is married in this version, and she's cheating on him with Paul. Lee will also accompany Hyde in his nightly revels in London. Though hardly a moral figure, he is appalled by Hyde's behavior. Hyde carries out what is Jekyll's revenge by raping Jekyll's faithless wife, which leads to her death and the death of Paul (by python, no less). At the end, Hyde appears triumphant, having blamed all the murders on Jekyll who is alleged to have died in a fire that destroyed his home. This is the verdict of an inquest. But as Hyde is about to walk out of the courtroom scot free, the Jekyll side asserts itself and he turns back into Jekyll in full view of the police, who arrest him immediately. Good wins over evil in that Hyde's elaborate plans fail.

Compared to all these other film versions, *I Monster* is something of a mixed bag. It does follow Stevenson's story rather closely but, like many of the other versions, it wavers between a focus on the classic problem of good vs. evil in the human personality and a psychological interpretation along Freudian lines. The fundamental question then is, does the story deal with a moral conflict or a psychological one? Does the infamous drug give rise to the "sin within" (as the apostle Paul put it) or does it simply release the repressed side of a person which may not have a moral component at all? When Marlowe first gives the drug to a timid woman who then overtly expresses her sexual desires in a promiscuous way, one can see this as a moral transformation, evil replacing her good side. However, in the second instance, Marlowe gives the drug to an overbearing man who becomes emotional and tender, which seems to suggest simply a psychological change rather than a moral one.

The film does imply, especially in the opening dialogue between Marlowe and his friends, that the opinion that humans are basically good is fatally flawed. The idea that human life is only really restricted by repression (*à la* Freud) is equally false. This is similar to the Mamoulian version of the story where Hyde morphs from a caveman like character into a purely evil one. However, like that earlier version, the film seems to waver back and forth between those two views. Part of this may be due to its first-time director, 22-year-old Stephen Weeks, whom Lee had recommended. The film was made by Hammer's rival, Amicus, which did not have the same production resources as Hammer.

Mamoulian's film attempts to move from the psychological repression view to Hyde as evil incarnate step by step, complete with religious imagery but, as stated above, without complete success. In *I Monster,* the two themes more just overlay each other with Marlowe quickly going from the psychological to the moral and spiritual emphasis. There is abundant religious imagery but it never really goes anywhere. Fredric March's Jekyll prays to God, confessing that he has trampled on His domain. This represents at least an attempt at moving from a psychological interpretation of the story to Stevenson's original emphasis on the "sin within." While Mamoulian's version is not completely successful in this, *I Monster* is less so since Marlowe's embracing of the reality of evil is not clearly delineated. The religious elements are never really integrated into the story. Is there a point to having the Salvation Army playing a hymn like "Jesus Shall Reign" as Marlowe is being taken over by Blake in the park scene? Is this intended to be ironic? We don't really know.

Lee is impressive as Marlowe. He registers a number of reactions in the earlier scenes of the film. He is alternately hesitant, inquisitive and assertive. He is completely convincing as someone forging ahead into unknown territory, not certain what the results will be. The character as written is not as effective in the transition from the psychological to the moral and spiritual. But Lee does his best to make it credible, especially when Marlowe realizes he is dealing with the ugliness of evil.

It is however in the role of Blake that his performance falters. Blake operates on a single note throughout. He can appear fearsome, especially when he is stalking the tavern woman. Yet Blake is essentially just a sadistic and sinister figure. Lee's portrayal lacks the initial welcoming character of a Dracula or the essential sadness of the Creature or even Kharis in *The Mummy.* We are not given the opportunity to care about either Marlowe or Blake. Neither one is really an engaging character. The reasons for this are multiple. They result in part from the script and the direction. In addition, however, there appears to be a lack of intensity, for want of a better term, in Lee's performance. At this point in his career, he had been appearing in so-called "horror films" for 15 years. His best films at Hammer were behind him. He would soon broaden out into everything from James Bond (*The Man With the Golden Gun*) to *The Three Musketeers* (adding to the costume adventures he did for Hammer). There may have been something of a lack of interest on his part at this stage.

Yet, as we will see, Lee was not finished with the horror film. He was able to rebound from this film for some striking performances in Hammer films. Also, Saruman and Count Dooku awaited on the horizon.

11

Horror Express (1972)

The Context of the Film

Horror Express (1972) was a Spanish-English production that reunited the two horror film stalwarts, Christopher Lee and Peter Cushing. This was essentially a Spanish B film whose commercial prospects in the English-speaking world were guaranteed by the presence of Cushing and Lee. The film points forward to major changes in the whole genre of horror itself.

By 1972, Hammer was in serious decline. More and more of their films were based on exploitation and less on story and imagination. Under the leadership of Michael Carreras who took over from his father Sir James, this had become painfully evident. Its first appearance was in the 1970 film *The Vampire Lovers*, based on J. Sheridan LeFanu's vampire novella *Carmilla*. A joint production of Hammer and American International (the company which had done the Vincent Price–Edgar Allan Poe films), it featured gratuitous nudity. Nudity unfortunately became the defining mark of a number of later Hammer features including the *Vampire Lovers* sequels (*Lust for a Vampire* and *Twins of Evil*), *Countess Dracula* and *Vampire Circus*. Martine Beswick, one of the "Hammer Glamour" girls in that era, said in a video interview that such a preponderance of nudity threw off Hammer's whole focus. She herself had two brief nude scenes in the interesting *Dr. Jekyll and Sister Hyde* but she pointed out that those scenes were integral to the story and both very brief. Hammer at this point was looking more like a progression of "Playboy Meets the Monsters" (the real-life twins in *Twins of Evil*, Madeline and Mary Collison, had posed together for *Playboy*).

Hammer's best work was behind them. Christopher Lee at this point was far from happy with Hammer's direction and increasingly pointless Dracula sequels. He maintained that he was emotionally blackmailed into doing them by Michael Carreras, who insisted that he (Lee) would put people out of work by declining to star in them. (Lee's presence was essential to getting the necessary financing.) Peter Cushing and Lee at this point were no longer the marquee players which they had been earlier. Both would move on to more meaningful roles in everything from James Bond to *Star Wars.*

Horror Express was a transition point for them. The film at least avoided the excesses of the later Hammers.

The Film

The film opens with a voiceover introduction by Professor Alexander Saxton (Lee). He refers to a disastrous event that occurred related to a Royal Geological Society expedition which he led in Manchuria, China. The full story is then shown in flashback. Prof. Saxton believes that he has found the remains of a primitive man dating back millions of years. He arranges to have what he calls a "fossil" shipped back to England with him. The first leg of the journey will be on the Trans-Siberian Express. At the train station, Saxton meets a colleague, Dr. Wells (Peter Cushing), who is curious about the large box that Saxton is transporting.

On the train, there's an intriguing assortment of passengers. Count and Countess Petrovski (George Rigaud, Silvia Tortosa) are traveling with their "spiritual advisor," a Russian monk named Father Pujardov. There is an attractive woman traveling alone named Natasha (Helga Line) and last, but by no means least, a police inspector (Julio Pena).

A thief is found dead next to the box with his eyes completely white. The assumption is that he was blind but that proves unconvincing given the fact that he was able to move about the platform. This also wouldn't explain the whiteness of his eyes. A police inspector and the two scientists are baffled.

Dr. Wells is not the only passenger intrigued by Saxton's large box. Father Pujardov maintains that there is something evil about its contents. He uses a piece of chalk to demonstrate that he cannot make the sign of the cross on the box. The cross cannot be in the presence of evil. He shows that he has no difficulty making the sign of the cross on the train platform itself. Saxton dismisses all this as utter nonsense. The passengers board the train and it departs.

Dr. Wells is anxious to know what is in the box and Saxton's refusal to tell him only increases his curiosity. He bribes the porter to open the box so he will be able to see what is inside. The porter assures himself that he is alone in the luggage car and then proceeds to open the box. A hairy hand reaches out and kills him. He collapses on the floor with his eyes all-white. The inhabitant in the box not only appears to be a monster but seems intelligent enough to pick the lock and break out of its confinement. Wells returns to find the porter dead and the thing in the box missing.

Saxton insists that the creature cannot be alive since it is, in his belief, millions of years old. Yet he cannot dispute the reality of the evidence before him.. He conjectures that the caveman may have been in a state of suspended animation. This hardly satisfies Wells. Other victims are found on the train, dead with their eyes whited out. This includes the woman Natasha, who is discovered to have been a spy. The police inspector wants to avoid creating a panic on the train. The two scientists perform an autopsy on one of the victims only to learn that the dead person's brain has become completely smooth. The creature has somehow absorbed the knowledge of its victims. The monster is finally gunned down by the police inspector and it would appear that the threat has ended. When Saxton and Wells investigate the eyes of the creature, they find its last living image is of the police inspector. They also find to their astonishment images of a prehistoric Earth seen from outer space. They conclude that this is no prehistoric caveman but an alien who came to Earth millions of years ago.

What is even more disturbing is that the murders continue. The alien has taken on a new body in the form of the police inspector. Father Pujardov tries to warn the count and countess that there is something evil on the train. To underscore his point, a religious painting in their luxury compartment crashes to the floor for no reason. Pujardov then confronts the inspector, who is now possessed. Inexplicitly, instead of opposing what he sees as the influence of Satan, the monk now pledges himself into what he believes is the Devil's service. In some unrevealed sense, he may be seeking the power which he believes the demonic inspector now has.

Word of the murders is wired to the Russian authorities. At the next stop the train is bordered by a military captain named Kazan (Telly Savalas). Kazan thinks the only problem is that there are rebels on the train. Meanwhile, the creature has absorbed the brains of the count and an engineer, killing them. The creature is in fact importing all the content of the brains of its victims. Saxton has come to the conclusion that light affects the creature. When the lights are extinguished, the creature's red eyes are seen in whomever it has inhabited. This identifies the police inspector as the current "host" of the alien. Kazan shoots the inspector but the alien then transfers itself into the monk, who kills all of Kazan's men.

Saxton has confirmed that the creature loses its power when confronted with light. Using bright light, he and Wells keep the creature from killing the countess and force it to reveal itself. It tells them that it is an alien form of energy which came to Earth as part of an expedition millions of years ago. It was left behind by accident and can only survive by inhabiting other life forms. The creature has been absorbing the information in the brains of its victims in order to find a way to escape back into space. The creature tries to negotiate for its freedom by offering to give Saxton its advanced knowledge in science, technology and medicine. Saxton pauses, admittedly intrigued by the alien's offer.

The offer is just a ruse. We learn now that the alien has other, more disturbing powers. It also is able to raise the dead and command them to do its bidding. The creature proceeds to reanimate the count, who attacks Saxton. Saxton, bringing the terrified countess with him, flees the creature and the revived count. The creature in turns reanimates all of its victims who now, as white-eyed zombies, march on the remaining passengers. The train station having been alerted that the events on the train may be part of a war, switches the rails so that it will plunge into an abyss, killing all on board. Saxton and Wells get all the remaining passengers into the last train car. They manage to unhook the car just before the zombies get to them. The rest of the train, now derailed, crashes down a cliff. The caboose manages to stop just short of the edge of the cliff. Presumably now all have died including the alien. As Saxton and Wells look down at the burning remains of the train the film comes to an end.

Dr. Wells (Peter Cushing, left) confers with fellow scientist Prof. Saxton (Christopher Lee) in *Horror Express* (1973).

Key Themes

At first glance, *Horror Express* can seem undistinguished from a host of low-budget horror films of this period (*The Abominable Dr. Phibes, Count Yorga, Blacula*). Yet despite the fact that it seems a lesser horror entry compared with the earlier Hammer films, it features a number of themes that would prove to be very influential later. As we will see however, these influences are not necessarily positive. A key element which would be much more evident in the following year's *The Exorcist* is the failure of Christian figures to be able to confront, much less overcome, the forces of evil. Hammer had led the way in this disturbing trend in their film *Scars of Dracula* (1970) with Christopher Lee in the title role. In this film, Michael Gwynn plays a priest who is no match for the vampire bats unleashed by Dracula. He and many of his parishioners are all killed in a church, no less. This is a far cry from Van Helsing or the Duc de Richleau. (We will see in a subsequent chapter that at the very end Hammer was able to modify this a bit with Peter Cushing returning in a Van Helsing role.)

The portrayal of Father Pujardov is an example of this diminished religious figure. While there are serious questions about his character, his role in the film evidences a basic confusion in the screenplay. Initially Pujardov is convinced that the contents of Saxton's box are satanic. To demonstrate this, he shows that, while he can make the sign of the cross on the train platform in chalk, he cannot do so with the box. As noted above, the monk's explanation is that the cross cannot be present where there is something evil. In a later scene an engineer raises this same question. He can give no scientific reason for why the chalk could not leave a mark on the box. In a scene in the count and countess' state room, a religious picture mysteriously crashes to the floor.

The first question we are left with is the nature of the creature. Is it an extra-terrestrial or is it, as Father Pujardov claims, a demon? If it is an alien then how does the film account for the chalk not being able to make the sign of the cross or the picture suddenly falling off the wall? This is not the only confusing point. Why does Father Pujardov—who appears to have his concerns validated by the murders on the train—suddenly pledge himself to this evil being? Is he really a monk? We only know that he has been retained by the count and countess as their "spiritual advisor." Was the chalk a trick on his part, along with the fallen picture?

None of these issues are addressed in the film itself. The fact remains that this often confused and indeed confusing aspect of the spiritual nature of good *and* evil has become a staple in horror films. In *Black Christmas*

(1974), there is an evil presence in a sorority house but it is never explained. Priests are helpless in *The Omen* (1976). Michael Myers appears and disappears at will in the *Halloween* series. This uncertain aspect of the supernatural exists up to the present day in the *Conjuring* and *Paranormal* film series. *Horror Express* is not the first example of this tendency but it is certainly a prominent one.

The creature's victims are reanimated and march on the living. Going back to *Night of the Living Dead* (1968), the zombie motif is very much still with us as the success of a television series like *The Walking Dead* demonstrates. If one accepts the stated premise of the creature itself, that it is an alien with the power to raise the dead, then we have one of the central themes of George Romero's zombie films. Somehow these mindless walking dead beings are the result of something that has come out of space. While this film along with Romero's *Living Dead* series popularized this now dominant idea, the theme has a long history going back to the inept (albeit hilarious) Edward D. Wood classic *Plan 9 from Outer Space* (1958).

Another theme that has become a cliché: the "Is-it-really-over?" motif. Whereas classic horror films up to and including Hammer's golden age always ended on a decisive note, that is not the case in what could be termed the post-modern horror film of which *Horror Express* is an early and notable example. In the older films, the Frankenstein Monster, Dracula, the werewolf, the Mummy (or whatever) was destroyed at the conclusion of the film. Granted the monster was invariably revived in a sequel, the individual films nearly always ended unambiguously with the death of its creature.

Horror Express ends with a fiery conflagration. The assumption is that the creature and all of its zombie followers have perished. Yet how can we be sure? The alien has been full of surprises. What if Father Pujardov's concerns were correct? Suppose the creature is not an alien but a demon. In the Bible, the origin of Satan and his fallen angels predate the Creation. The creature's images of Earth could have come from this early stage of Creation. If the creature is some form of demon, are we certain that even fire can destroy it? If the creature has survived for millions of years, it is certainly possible that it survived the train wreck.

This sort of ambivalent ending has been with us for over 40 years. As far back as 1972, an example was seen in an otherwise forgettable television version of *The Hound of the Baskervilles*. After the hound and Stapleton have been killed and the mystery explained, the howl of the hound is heard yet again. Watson asks, "What is it?" Holmes replies, "It is just the wind." Right! This whole trend weakens one of the strongest themes in the horror story tradition: the certainty that good will eventually triumph over evil. Evil is not invincible. Yet this has been clearly the tendency in the horror film for many years now. It appears that other forms of myth and fantasy have replaced the somewhat nihilistic emphasis of horror. There has been no more fearful looking monster in the films of the post-modern period than the creature in *Alien.* Yet that creature is not indestructible. The classic conflict of good vs. evil has been more effectively explored in *Lord of the Rings* and *Star Wars.* It is striking to note that both Cushing and Lee gave memorable performances in these film series.

Christopher Lee: Professor Sir Alexander Saxton

Our first exposure to Professor Saxton is the voiceover that introduces the film. We learn two important things here. First that a "disaster" has occurred and, second, that Saxton accepts responsibility for it. This opening statement jars with our first actual introduction to Saxton. His entire focus is on his "fossil" which is concealed in an enormous wooden box. Saxton is intensely jealous of his find. This applies to a colleague like Dr. Wells or to the monk Father Pujardov, whose concerns about Satan are dismisses as rubbish by Saxton.

Lee invests Saxton with an arrogant, close-minded attitude. Yet a critical dimension of his role is his pride in being a scientist. Once the creature escapes and goes on a murderous rampage, Saxton has to use his same scientific approach to understand what is taking place. With Wells' help, he performs autopsies on several victims. He emerges as a scientific detective. He is probing, studying, trying to find out what is going on.

Lee is able to combine both the positive and negative aspects of the role effectively. He is proud, even arrogant at first. Yet this is not totally surprising given the fact that he has found what he believes to be the greatest discovery of his career. His confidence is in his scientific knowledge and training. When he is forced to realize that his so-called fossil is really alive and indeed dangerous, he brings that same scientific background to the question of what the creature is and how to stop it.

A critical point in Lee's performance occurs when the alien now inside Father Pujardov's body offers to give Saxton knowledge he could only dream of obtaining. At this moment, Saxton falters. Yet he would not be a scientist if he were not at least intrigued by the idea of information that could be able to cure diseases. As it turns out, the creature is simply playing for time (which also would fit the description of a demon). Saxton, suddenly attacked by the reanimated count, now grasps the full reality of the situation. There is no possibility of bargaining with the alien. The creature's power to resurrect his victims as zombies makes it more dangerous. This reality ends the phase of Saxton's studying and analyzing the alien. It is now time for action. At this point, Saxton and Wells don't know that the train is being detoured off the main track to its destruction. They do know that everyone is in danger of the zombie rampage. Saxton becomes a man of action and of courage. He brings the countess with him. The surviving passengers are gathered together in the last car. Their safety demands that they unhook that car from the rest of the train. With Wells' help, Saxton does this. They are saved as the rest of the train goes over the cliff.

Saxton has gone through a transformation. From being initially egocentric and intolerant, he emerges as something of a hero. In the midst of a frantic and deadly situation, he adjusts and changes as events dictate. He never loses his pose as the "scientist." This is what makes him vulnerable to the alleged offer of knowledge from the alien. There is also an echo here of the Adam and Eve story in the Bible where the serpent offers them special knowledge.

The attack of the reanimated count galvanizes Saxton into action. There is a condescending air about him at first. He is fixated on his discovery. In the later moment of crisis, his expression becomes resolute and determined. The same determination that led to the discovery of the creature now is directed toward its destruction. Lee conveys this through facial expressions more than anything else.

Professor Saxton was not a great role for Lee. It was, however, a significant one. The script does give him a motivation for change (which it doesn't for Father Pujardov). He is able to carry this out by the way he interacts with the people around him. Much of this is conveyed through his expressive eyes, which set him off from the victims whose eyes are whited out. The same traits that walled him off from people (whom at the time he saw as being inferior), later bring him to the place of delivering the surviving passengers from the threat of the zombies and the train crash. Professor Saxton is not an in-depth character, but Lee's portrayal makes him interesting and, in the end, sympathetic.

The Satanic Rites
of Dracula (1973)

Christopher Lee was unhappy with his final performance as Count Dracula. He made it clear he was appearing in the film under protest. However, *The Satanic Rites of Dracula* has some notable features which make it far superior to its immediate predecessors. It merits consideration as the last time Lee essayed his greatest role and the last time he did battle with his old nemesis Van Helsing, played of course by Peter Cushing.

Context of the Film

In the 1970s, Hammer Films kept trying to recycle their initially inventive approach to Gothic horror with more and more exploitative efforts. Following the fairly interesting *Taste the Blood of Dracula* (1970), which at least had the distinction of bringing Dracula to England, there seemed nowhere else to go with the series. After five films, four of which included Lee as the count, it appeared that the subject had been fully covered. To Lee's chagrin, much of Bram Stoker's actual novel had not been filmed. However, any real attempt to film the rambling novel with its many characters and journal entries seemed beyond the ability of filmmakers. The earliest film versions, F.W. Murnau's *Nosferatu* (1922) and Tod Browning's *Dracula*, had used the basic framework of the story and cut out many of the characters. Decades later, Francis Ford Coppola claimed to have filmed the novel as *Bram Stoker's Dracula* (1992) but the film was overlong and confusing. Hammer's original *Dracula*, to this day, remains the gold standard. *The Brides of Dracula* was a worthy sequel even without Lee, and *Dracula, Prince of Darkness* incorporated elements of the novel which had not been present in the 1958 original. By the time of *Taste the Blood of Dracula*, it seemed the series had run its course. The horror film was certainly changing. In 1968,

Hammer won the Queen's Award for Industry. Their future appeared bright. Yet three films made that year altered the horror film genre forever: *Rosemary's Baby, Night of the Living Dead* and *Witchfinder General* (*Conqueror Worm* in the U.S.). In various ways these films were darker and more violent than horror films had been up to this period. The standard resolution of good defeating the power of was no longer a given. These films had a nihilistic quality summarized by the toast at the conclusion of *Rosemary's Baby*: "God is dead! Long live Satan!"

The year 1968 was among the most turbulent in the twentieth century with the Vietnam War, the Soviet invasion of Czechoslovakia and student protests around the globe. It was the year of the assassinations of Martin Luther King and Robert Kennedy.

Yet if we think of the horror film as a kind of spiritual barometer of the culture (as stated in Siegfried Kracauer's major work *From Caligari to Hitler*), these events alone do not tell the whole story. The "death of God" movement of a few years earlier symbolized a significant switch in Western values. Confidence in traditional beliefs and institutions beginning with the church and the government had diminished. This would accelerate with everything from Watergate to a greater explicitness in film and the arts in general. In short, the sort of basic value system that was assumed in the earlier Hammer films had deteriorated. For all the concerns of violence and sexuality in those earlier films, their basic outlook was essentially traditional. This could be seen in a director like Terence Fisher, who confidently proclaimed his conviction that good would always triumph over evil. With the coming of *Star Wars*, there would be a rebirth of myth and mysticism. However, the "Force" represented a different view of spirituality than that found in the historic Christianity represented by Van Helsing and the whole earlier Hammer tradition. (Hammer's two main stars, Cushing and Lee, would be part of this new mythology with Lee appearing in both the *Star Wars* and *Lord of the Rings* series.) These films recaptured the triumph of good over evil in a new and different form. On the other hand, the horror film itself only became more nihilistic as the new horror franchises indicated (*Halloween, Friday the Thirteenth, Nightmare on Elm Street*). Hammer was caught between these two trends.

It is unfortunate that as Hammer was trying to find its way in the 1970s, they didn't tap into the works of J.R.R. Tolkien (*The Hobbit, The Lord of the Rings*) or C.S. Lewis (*The Chronicles of Narnia, Out of the Silent Planet, Perelandra, That Hideous Strength*). By the 1970s, the horror film was moving more into the area of the occult. Hammer had entered that realm with the highly successful *The Devil Rides Out*, which had also appeared in 1968. Lee was interested in Wheatley's works and suggested that this was a direction Hammer might follow. But Hammer did not film another Wheatley occult thriller until 1976's *To the Devil a Daughter,* with very mixed results.

Hammer basically was caught between its traditional film staples like Dracula and Frankenstein and the changes that were taking place not only in horror but in film in general. Right after *Taste the Blood of Dracula* they produced *Scars of Dracula,* which at first glance appeared to be a re-telling of the original story, as though Hammer was starting all over again. That was hardly the case as they seemed to be diving uncritically into the emerging tendencies in the horror film. *Scars of Dracula* has gratuitous nudity, sadism and a priest who is powerless against the forces of evil. According to Phil Hardy's *The Overlook Film Encyclopedia: Horror,* this is a film which shows contempt for its audience. That sums it up as the film throws out most of what we have seen in Hammer Draculas up to this point. Hammer next tried to bring Dracula into the present day with *Dracula A.D. 1972.* The film, directed by newcomer Alan Gibson, was embarrassing as Dracula now deals with 1970s teenagers. No wonder Lee was frustrated. Ironically, the best part of the film was a climactic confrontation between Van Helsing and Dracula in an abandoned church. This scene could just as easily have been set in the Victorian period.

In spite of these setbacks and embarrassments, Hammer was not done with Dracula. They managed to persuade Lee to give one last performance in the series. Cushing was once again signed on to play Van Helsing in a contemporary setting (this Van Helsing is the grandson of the Victorian spiritual champion but is essentially the same character given Cushing's portrayal). The initial title for the film was to be *Dracula Is Dead and Well and Living in London.* Lee called the film (retitled *The Satanic Rites of Dracula*) "fatuous, pointless, absurd."

Satanic Rites has some of the same problems as its predecessors, but it is a much better film. It successfully blends Hammer's classic approach with the new occult tendencies in horror. Warner Bros., which had produced *Dracula A.D. 1972,* was disenchanted and opted not to release *Satanic Rites* in the U.S. In 1978 the film was released by an independent distributor under the bland title of *Count Dracula and His Vampire Bride.* The film in an edited form was finally made available on video. This film, however, should not be dismissed. As the final appearance of Cushing and Lee in a Dracula film, it merits consideration. Even beyond this, it is one of the best efforts of Hammer in the 1970s.

The Film

At a Black Mass, an Asian woman (Barbara Yu Ling) leads a group of four older men in hooded robes as she prepares to sacrifice of a naked young blonde woman. As this is taking place, we see a man (Maurice O'Connell) bound and gagged in a room above where the ceremony is taking place. He is able to work his way out of his ropes and then attacks his guard. The man tries to sneak out of the house but he crosses an electric eye signal which gives out a warning. Pursued by two men on motorcycles, he is seriously injured but manages finally to get away.

This man, an undercover British police officer named Hanson, has gathered data on events taking place in a remote estate called Pelham House. He has taken a number of slides showing five figures who have frequented the house. But he dies from his injuries before he can give all the details. His work is part of an investigation into four prominent men who are allegedly involved in some form of black magic. This involvement would presumably create the possibility of blackmail, leading to security leaks. His superiors review the slides that Hanson and identify four prominent citizens, including Nobel Prize winner Julian Keeley (Freddie Jones). The fifth slide shows the door to the house but no one is in the picture. They conclude that Hanson was mistaken in identifying five individuals entering the house. Of course, we will realize that *they* are the ones who are wrong

A special officer named Murray (Michael Coles) has some knowledge of occult practices. Reviewing the evidence that Hanson compiled, Murray feels the need to call in an expert on witchcraft and the occult. The expert, not surprisingly, is Dr. Lorrimer Van Helsing (Peter Cushing), grandson of the original Abraham Van Helsing. When Lorrimer sees the evidence, he is convinced that something very serious is taking place. Lorrimer has known Julian Keeley since college. Lorrimer claims

Lee in his final performance as Count Dracula in *The Satanic Rites of Dracula* (1973).

that his granddaughter Jessica Van Helsing (Joanna Lumley, the Bond Girl in 1969's *On Her Majesty's Secret Service*) is a valuable assistant in his research. A member of the group, Jane (Valerie Van Ost), is abducted by the same motorcycle duo who had pursued Hanson.

Lorrimer Van Helsing pays an unannounced visit to his old friend Professor Keeley and finds him extremely agitated. Keeley is conducting an experiment for a rich, reclusive industrialist named D.D. Denham. His research is focused on the virus that caused the Black Plague of the Middle Ages. As Van Helsing looks over Keeley's work, he realizes that, instead of trying to eliminate the virus, Keeley is trying to strengthen it. The result would be a super-virus that could destroy all life on Earth. When Van Helsing confronts him, Keeley says he had to obey Denham's orders. A motorcycle guard enters and fires his gun at Van Helsing; the bullet grazes him and renders him unconscious. When he awakens, he sees the hanged body of Keeley swinging from the ceiling.

Murray and another special agent, Torrance (William Franklyn), decide to investigate Pelham House, and Jessica insists on along with them. At the entranceway to the strange house, Murray tells her to remain in the car and "keep quiet." Murray and Torrance are invited in and are introduced to Chin Yang, the Asian woman who led the Black Mass at the beginning of the film. The two agents rather awkwardly explain their presence by saying that some neighbors had complained of strange noises the night before. The woman counters that Pelham House is in an isolated location. What neighbors? They try to say that sound can travel on a clear night. The woman is obviously suspicious.

Jessica has snuck into the house to do her own investigation. In a cellar, she finds Jane, the abducted female assistant, chained to a wall. She has blood on her. Jessica attempts to set her free but then realizes that Jane has become a vampire. Other vampire women emerge and Jessica is terrified. (The women represent various races as though Hammer was politically correct in casting its vampire women. The earlier *Vampire Lovers* had featured five women, all white.) Jessica's screams bring Murray and Torrance running to her rescue. Murray fashions a stake from a wooden box and kills Jane. The other women cower as the men and Jessica escape.

Van Helsing learns of the vampire threat and suspects that Dracula is behind all this. In a few days there will be the celebration of the Witches' Sabbat. Torrance speculates that if Dracula's intention is to release the Black Plague, humanity will eventually die and Dracula will be left with no more source for human blood. "Why would Dracula do this?" he asks. Van Helsing responds that this may be an ultimate death wish for the vampire king, perhaps the only way he can find any lasting peace.

Van Helsing, suspicious that the recluse Denham is in fact Dracula, goes to the headquarters of his company. When told that no one may visit Denham, Van Helsing simply says, "Tell him who I am and I'm sure he will see me." Before the guard can do so, the phone rings with instructions to let Van Helsing go up to Denham's private suite.

Van Helsing is totally prepared. He has a crucifix as well as a gun with a silver bullet made from a cross. He quickly learns that his suspicions are correct and that the mysterious Denham is in reality Count Dracula. But before he can fire his silver bullet, one of Dracula's henchmen enters and disarms him.

Jessica has also been captured and Van Helsing learns to his horror that she is to be made Dracula's consort at the height of the Black Mass. Dracula tells Van Helsing that he is to take the place of the hanged Keeley. Van Helsing along with the three "disciples" will be the carriers of the plague to the world. Dracula pronounces that they will be his Four Horsemen of the Apocalypse. In one of the few lines taken from Stoker's novel, Dracula states that this will be his ultimate revenge.

The three men protest that this was not what they were promised. Of course, Dracula tricked them. He hypnotizes the first follower, who then breaks the vial of the plague which Dracula has previously handed out. The man immediately feels agonizing pain. Unbeknownst to all involved with the ritual, Murray has managed to enter the house through the basement. Confronted by the vampire women, he remembers that one of the ways to destroy a vampire is by running water (which was how Dracula was destroyed in *Dracula, Prince of Darkness*). He turns on a sprinkler system which douses the women, destroying them. In a fight with a motorcycle guard, Murray forces him onto an electric control panel which bursts into flame.

The whole building begins to burn. As the flames rise, Van Helsing tells Murray to save his unconscious granddaughter. Dracula's focus now is on Van Helsing so he makes no attempt to stop Murray. A key element in Dracula's revenge is the elimination of Van Helsing. But this Van Helsing lacks none of the acrobatics of his ancestor who, in *Dracula*, ran down the length of a banquet table, leaped into the air and pulled down a heavy set of curtains letting the sun into the room and destroying Dracula. This Van Helsing proceeds to leap through a window to get out of the burning building. Van Helsing realizes that outside on the grounds is a Hawthorne tree whose branches were allegedly used to make Christ's crown of thorns. Exposure to the thorns of this tree has essentially the same effect as the symbol of the cross. Van Helsing calls out to Dracula, who follows after him and gets caught in the

Dracula (Christopher Lee) in the fiery finale of *The Satanic Rites of Dracula* (1973).

tree. Now Van Helsing takes a post from a wooden fence and, using it as a stake, plunges it into Dracula's heart. For the last time, Lee's Dracula dissolves into dust.

Key Themes

Satanic Rites is not free from the exploitative aspects of the Hammer films of this period. To begin with, there is more nudity than is necessary, especially when related to violence (the staking of Jane) or the Black Mass as at the beginning of the film. Later video editions excised these scenes. There are more than a few contrivances. Sharp pieces of wood somehow always seem to be close at hand whenever anyone is trying to kill a vampire. It is disturbing to note that Dracula's ghastly plan almost succeeds. If the guard in the fight at the climax had not touched the electric panel with a piece of metal, the fire which enabled the principals to escape would not have started.

Finally Dracula knows better than anyone what can destroy him. He has his followers operating out of Pelham House and he never notices the Hawthorne Bush nearby? It would only take a minute to order a groundskeeper or even one of the motorcycle assassins to take it down!

Even with these drawbacks, the film succeeds in a number of key areas. An obvious point was the reunion of Cushing and Lee as Van Helsing and Dracula respectively (a union which almost saved *Dracula A.D. 1972* but not quite). The film does succeed in bringing together the current (1974) focus on the occult with classic Gothic horror. Parallels between Dracula and Satan were present in Hammer's series all the way back to *Dracula, Prince of Darkness*. Here it is made explicit. In addition, giving Dracula a goal that is far more than seeking some kind of revenge or some enticing female victim raises the theme to a new level. Dracula here intends to destroy the world. This is a mission worthy of Satan himself. Such a mission represents Dracula's revenge not simply against Van Helsing and his allies but it is a revenge against the whole world. It is finally a revenge against life itself since life is something Dracula, the Undead, can never really have.

Another effective point is placing Dracula not in some castle or abandoned church but in a very modern high-rise building. There is also the suggestion of wealthy land owners sucking away the life of ordinary people. Hammer had always shown evil aristocrats in their films. Here we have the modern-day equivalent of those with power intending to dominate everyone else. Dracula's tool of destruction is not to unleash a horde of vampire bats or turn unsuspecting individuals into human vampires. It is to spread a plague that will kill everyone. This film was made years before the outbreak of AIDS or the appearance of the Zika virus. The idea of Dracula's ultimate revenge being a worldwide plague is innovative and striking.

Finally, this film does not have a weak or ineffectual Christian representative. Cushing's Van Helsing is as memorable as ever. He has a variety of means of destroying Dracula (even if the reference to silver seems to have been borrowed from a werewolf film). Dracula's destruction in the Hawthorne Bush is also a fresh idea; I do not recall the Hawthorne Bush being mentioned in any previous Hammer film.

Satanic Rites is by no means a great film but it *is* a worthy entry among the later Hammer efforts. It does offer some fresh ideas on its well-worn theme. It also embraces the theme of the occult without losing its central Gothic focus—and in so doing, it echoes one of Hammer's greatest films, *The Devil Rides Out*. Finally, this was the last time Christopher Lee played the role of Dracula.

Christopher Lee—Farewell to Dracula

In spite of Lee's many reservations about *Satanic Rites*, it is a fitting end to his long career of playing the role (which also included a 1970 Spanish film entitled *Count Dracula*). Given his familiarity with the part and his unfortunate disdain for the way he was pressured to play it yet again, he could have simply walked through his performance. Lee never did that in any of his previous portrayals and he certainly does not do it here. There are additional touches he brings to the role. It is interesting that he affects an almost Bela Lugosi–like accent when Van Helsing visits him. As Van Helsing and the others speculate as to why Dracula would be seeking the destruction of the human race, Lee's facial expression captures the sense of a weary count. It has all gone on too long for him. At the same time, he has lost none of his grandiosity. To interfere with God's plans for humanity he nurtures his own apocalyptic designs. Lee is able to alternate between this sense of resignation and equal determination to have his final revenge.

Also given special emphasis: his fierce antagonism to Van Helsing who, after all, is his greatest nemesis. He positively delights in the perverse idea that he will make Van Helsing's granddaughter his permanent consort. He relishes the fact that Van Helsing will be compelled to witness this. When everything is going up in a blaze, he turns his attention solely to Van Helsing. When Van Helsing cries out (in effect) "Come and get me," Dracula never hesitates. He falls into the trap. This may certainly seem a contrivance but the fury on Dracula's face communicates the fact that he wants nothing more than to do away with his enemy. Once caught in the bush, Lee performs like a trapped animal. He twists and turns trying to break free, desperation written all over his face. Scratched and bruised, he cries out in anger and pain. Lee has done seven death scenes as Dracula. Yet each one of them is memorable in its own way. Dracula is unrepentant to the end. He never asks for mercy. As the personification of evil, he cannot be redeemed. He can only be destroyed. Dracula truly is dead but Lee's many performances in the role will be remembered for years to come.

13

The Man with
the Golden Gun (1974)

Context of the Film

By 1974, Lee was largely done with Hammer. As we have seen, Hammer was running out of ideas and imagination by the 1970s. One of their most bizarre moves was a partnership with the Shaw Brothers who specialized in kung fu films. The mind-boggling result was a travesty called *The Legend of the Seven Golden Vampires*. Peter Cushing mustered as much dignity as he could playing Van Helsing once again. Fortunately for him, he would begin work on *Star Wars* in two years. But by then, Lee had had it, sick to death with what Hammer was doing to Dracula. With a script that was essentially "Dracula Goes to Hong Kong," he bowed out. The part of Dracula was played by John Forbes-Robertson, who had a small part in *The Vampire Lovers*. With the release of *The Exorcist,* it was clear that the horror film was going in a very different direction from that of the original Gothic classics, *Frankenstein* and *Dracula*. Lee had established an international reputation from both Hammer and horror films in general. He was now in a position to go in a new career direction. One example of that was the enormously successful James Bond series. In 1973, Lee was cast in the title role in *The Man with the Golden Gun.*

Golden Gun was the ninth James Bond film and the last to be co-produced by Albert R. Broccoli and Harry Saltzman. The first Bond film, *Dr. No,* starred Sean Connery as Bond and was released in 1962. The Bond novels and short stories had been written by Ian Fleming and were enormously successful. The Bond films however brought the character to a much wider audience, making British Secret Service agent James Bond a cultural icon. His code number 007 (signifying a license to kill) became easily recognized throughout the world. Interestingly, Christopher Lee was a distant relative to Ian Fleming and apparently Fleming had suggested Lee for the role of the first villain in the series, Dr. No. That was not to be; but by the time of *Golden Gun,* the opportunity was ripe for Lee to play a major role in the series. Bond was played for the second time by British actor Roger Moore. The co-star in the film, Britt Ekland, had just appeared with Lee in *The Wicker Man.* This film would have none of the intensity of that classic. As it would turn out, Lee was the most memorable part of the picture.

The Film

The British Secret Service (MI6) receives a golden bullet with Bond's code number, 007, on it. The head of the service, "M," believes that this is a warning from the feared assassin Francisco Scaramanga (Lee). His whereabouts are unknown and no one even knows what he looks like. His most telling physical characteristic is that he allegedly has three nipples on his chest. He reportedly charges one million dollars a killing. Scaramanga is sought throughout the world and supposedly is capable of killing anyone, anywhere, any time. His favorite weapon is a golden gun with gold bullets.

Given the threat that Scaramanga poses, M wants to take no chances. He orders Bond to go on leave. At this point, Bond has been on a special mission to aid a scientist named Gibson, who is trying to develop a plan for solar energy. Relieved of this assignment, Bond is not to be intimidated by Scaramanga. His search for the assassin leads him to Beirut where he learns that a belly dancer has one of Scaramanga's golden bullets in her navel. Bond of course has little difficulty obtaining it. He learns that the manufacturers of the golden bullets take them to a casino where a mysterious woman picks them up. The woman in question, Andrea Anders (Maud Adams), turns out to be Scaramanga's mistress and accomplice,. Bond trails her to Hong Kong.

At this point, an already convoluted plot becomes even more so. Bond's previous mission and the concern about Scaramanga come together when Bond discovers that Scaramanga's next victim is the solar energy scientist, Gibson. Bond also learns that the leaders of the British Secret Service are in Hong Kong and they want Bond back on the solar energy case. The reason is that a key part of Gibson's discovery, a small instrument called a Solex agitator, has apparently been stolen by one of Scaramanga's henchmen, a dwarf known as Nick Nack (played by Herve Villechaize who was the character Tattoo on the television series *Fantasy Island*). The idea of a notorious assassin having such a powerful tool in his possession is a serious concern. Assisting Bond in his work will be British agent Mary Goodnight (Britt Ekland).

Bond gets a lead that the "client" who paid Scaramanga to kill Gibson is a wealthy Bangkok industrialist whose business would suffer if solar energy became readily available. Believing that no one has ever seen Scaramanga, Bond pretends to be him, even showing a fake third nipple which he reveals to the industrialist Hai Fat (Richard Loo). But Bond however has miscalculated. Scaramanga is in fact a guest at Hai Fat's estate: Bond escapes with the aid of the police officer who had brought him to the MI6 temporary headquarters in Hong Kong. Scaramanga kills Hai Fat and takes over his empire. Scaramanga now has both the Solex agitator and the resources of Hai Fat.

Andrea comes to Bond's hotel and reveals that she sent the golden bullet with 007 on it to the British secret service in London. No one has a contract on Bond. In reality, she wants Bond to kill Scaramanga. In return, she promises to give Bond the Solex which she has stolen from Scaramanga. (The Solex is what Alfred Hitchcock would refer to as the MacGuffin, in other words, an object that everyone in the story is chasing after.) She will bring the Solex to a sports stadium the following day and give it to Bond once he has killed Scaramanga. (Bond does have a license to kill.)

As agreed, Bond comes to his seat in the stadium, right next to Andrea who seems to be staring blankly into space. There is an obvious reason for this. She is dead and Bond can see the trace of blood near her heart where the bullet entered. On Bond's other side is an elegant gentleman who reveals that he is Scaramanga and obviously was aware of Andrea's attempt to have him killed. It becomes apparent that Scaramanga views killing as something akin to a tennis match. He is laying down a challenge to Bond. Spotting the Solex next to Andrea's feet, Bond picks it up undetected and leaves the stadium. Outside, he gives it to Goodnight. They plan to put a homing device in Scaramanga's car. As Goodnight attempts to do this by opening the trunk, Scaramanga appears and locks *her* in the trunk.

Bond steals a car from a showroom and gives chase, knowing that Scaramanga now has both Goodnight and the Solex. What follows is a ridiculous car chase even by James Bond film standards. Bond is unintentionally joined by a vacationing Southern sherriff named J.W. Pepper (Clifton James). His presence may have been intended to provide some comic relief but he comes across as more annoying than funny. It turns out that Scaramanga has no shortage of gadgets. He affixes wings to his car and literally flies away.

Bond locates Scaramanga's island hideout by following Goodnight's tracking device. Scaramanga welcomes him and shows him that he is following up on the invention of solar energy himself. His elaborate laboratory includes a vat of liquid helium. Scaramanga demonstrates the power of his solar energy plant by targeting Bond's plane, which explodes into flames.

Bond also sees Goodnight in a bikini. It appears that she's being groomed to take the place of Scaramanga's former mistress.

One of the best scenes in the film has Scaramanga hosting a lunch for Bond and Goodnight. The meal is provided by Nick Nack. Scaramanga offers a toast to Bond and himself, claiming that they do identical work. In his view, they are both paid assassins. Bond strongly resents this. He replies that Scaramanga is a cold-blooded murderer for hire. His victims never have a chance. Bond on the other hand kills only in the line of duty to his government. Those he kills are usually killers themselves.

Scaramanga proposes that he and Bond have an old-fashioned duel. The weapons will be guns, Scaramanga brandishing his golden weapon while Bond has his standard service revolver. Bond has no choice but to agree. They stand back to back and march off 20 paces counted by Nick Nack. On 20, Bond turns rapidly and shoots—but Scaramanga has disappeared. Nick Nack offers to guide Bond, who is of course suspicious of the servant's motives.

This is not the first time that Scaramanga has had such a duel. Earlier in the film, another assassin had come looking for Scaramanga. The island

Christopher Lee as the assassin Scaramanga in the James Bond adventure *The Man with the Golden Gun* (1974).

headquarters has been set up like a giant circus funhouse. Pop-up figures representing everything from Wild West cowboys to gangsters emerge with fake guns blazing. There is even a life-size statue of Bond holding his gun. Bond is forced to play a cat-and-mouse game with Scaramanga in the midst of all this. As Scaramanga stalks Bond, he passes Bond's statue. The statue suddenly shoots him: Bond took the place of the statue and, with the element of surprise, killed his enemy. This is a nice ironic touch but hardly credible. Bond would have had to take the clothes off the statue, put them on and displace the statue all without making any noise or drawing any attention to himself. But improbable escapes are hardly new. Anyone who has ever seen a movie serial knows that, as do fans of "B" movies up to the present. There was a famous example in a Basil Rathbone Sherlock Holmes film where the title villain, the Spider Woman, has Holmes tied up inside a carnival shooting gallery., completely unaware of this, is outside shooting at the moving targets, one of which includes an unseen, bound-and-gagged Holmes. Somehow, every time Holmes' target comes around, Watson is distracted and fails to shoot. Eventually Holmes escapes. Of course.

Seeking to aid Bond Goodnight pushes one of Scaramanga's henchmen into the vat of liquid helium. This sets off a chain reaction. Bond and Goodnight escape in a boat before the whole island explodes. As they are making love (of course), it is revealed that Nick Nack is a stowaway. Bond easily dispatches him. The film ends with Bond and Goodnight in bed with M calling on the boat's telephone. When M asks for Goodnight, Bond simply replies "Good night," and hangs up. We wince.

Golden Gun is certainly one of the lesser Bond entries. It is, as the above summary indicates, overlong, confusing and contrived. It seems to be a paint-by-the-numbers entry in the series: beautiful women (check), car chases (check), big explosions (check), a master villain (check). Roger Moore is even more self-mocking in the role than his predecessor, Sean Connery.

But this below par Bond was a major step forward in Christopher Lee's career. Not only is he the best thing in the film, he emerges as one of the best Bond villains of all time. Up to this point, Lee was essentially only known for genre films, most of which were low-budget horror films. In this pre–*Star Wars* era, most horror, sci-fi and fantasy films were not taken seriously. Horror had entered the mainstream with *Rosemary's Baby* and *The Exorcist* and there had been a few serious science fiction films (*Planet of the Apes, 2001*), but by and large the entire fantasy genre was not viewed as having any kind of significant role in commercial film. *Golden Gun* at least introduced Lee to audiences that may not have seen him before.

Key Themes

While *The Man with the Golden Gun* is a major studio film, it also is very much a formula film, a commercial example of superficial entertainment. It is ironic that many of Lee's Hammer films (and his horror films in general) raise far more significant issues than a pure escapist film like *Golden Gun*. Classic Gothic horror deals with the essential struggle between good and evil, the nature of God, the afterlife, the soul and the spiritual realm in general. These larger issues are beyond the scope of a James Bond film, which just seeks to be an action thriller. Nonetheless, moral issues, if not spiritual ones, are invariably present, even in the background.

The most telling scene in the film is the lunch that Bond has with Scaramanga. Scaramanga's attempt to link himself with Bond as compatible killers is totally rejected by Bond. Scaramanga is on the surface amoral. He kills for pay. But he is not beyond seizing power for himself, as he does in his cold-blooded killing of the entrepreneur who hired him to kill the scientist. Scaramanga controls his entire world and seeks to maximize power for himself. Any threat, Andrea for example, is simply eliminated. He is therefore immoral. He represents power, ego and domination. He has no moral standard beyond himself. He is therefore a threat to everyone else. He finally is a threat to himself. We will discuss Lee's actual interpretation subsequently. For now, it is important to note that Bond's adversaries in this film (and in most others in the series) represent various types of megalomaniacs who have in reality defined most of twentieth century history. How else can one characterize Hitler, Stalin, Mao Tse Tung *et al.*?

These figures are not portrayed in Bond films as deranged madmen, much less monsters. They are invariably urbane, cultured and, to a degree, charming. They also represent the final outcome of ambition, power and pleasure. In reality, they are not totally unlike Lee's other villains like Count Dracula and Lord Summerisle. There is then a kind of warning that can at least be seen in these films even if it is only implied. The pursuit of standard goals can, if not restrained by some moral code, lead to evil and cruelty. There is of course nothing wrong with having ambitions or taking on challenges. Yet if these goals are not part of a large context, any one of us has the capacity to be a Scaramanga (or Dr. No or Goldfinger, etc.).

Bond himself is a morally compromised figure. He treats women as objects. He clearly has his own degree of pride and ambition. He can be cruel, even brutal. Yet Bond, in the tradition of "private eyes" like Sam Spade and Philip Marlowe, has a moral code which cannot be compromised. His goal goes beyond duty. Time and again he defies his superiors to overcome a threat they may not have perceived. Bond really is safeguarding the world. He is in effect a global police officer. He makes us draw a distinction between duty and morality. Duty can only go so far, Moral principles such as safeguarding human life or protecting the world from destruction cannot be reduced to a fixed set of rules and requirements. At the beginning of this film, Bond is told by his superiors to take a leave of absence for his own safety. Bond will not do this. His search for Scaramanga is not only for his own benefit. He rightly wants to investigate a deadly killer who is a threat to all.

This is why Bond objects so forcefully to Scaramanga's attempt to link the two of them. Yes, both are killers, but their motives are entirely different. For Scaramanga, human life is a commodity just like money. Given enough money (in his case a million dollars per hit), human life becomes of lesser value and can be eliminated. Bond's killings are designed to safeguard average people from the threat of domineering megalomaniacs. He does not always kill without ambiguity.

Scaramanga also kills for sport, as his duel with Bond shows. For Bond, killing may be necessary but it is no game. Nor will he kill unnecessarily. When he captures Nick Nack at the close of the film, he does not kill him. He simply ties him to the mast with the obvious intention of handing him over to the police.

This story has some interesting parallels with Richard Connell's famous short story "The Most Dangerous Game" which has been filmed numerous times, most notably in a 1932 version which used a set and several cast members from *King Kong*. The story focuses on Count Zaroff, a master hunter. Zaroff has become bored with hunting wild animals, which are no longer a challenge for him. He decides to begin hunting human beings. He has established himself on an island surrounded by reefs. Zaroff establishes misleading guides in the water that will cause boats to smash into the reefs. Zaroff gives a male survivor a head start and then proceeds to hunt him down. Invariably Zaroff kills his prey. The surviving female then become his possession, a trophy of the hunt.

The character of Scaramanga invites comparison to Count Zaroff. He has his island retreat. He doesn't kill his victims on the island (unless they come looking for him, as an earlier assailant does). But he views his killings as a kind of sport. In his mind, his duel with Bond is entirely fair and sporting. Once he has deposed of Bond, the bikini-clad Goodnight will remain as his "trophy." Zaroff finally comes to his end when he goes after a superior opponent (Joel McCrea in the 1932 film). The female "trophy" in that case was none other than Fay Wray, famous for *King Kong*.

Needless to say, it would be more than a little intriguing if Christopher

Lee had made a version of *The Most Dangerous Game*. His Scaramanga comes close enough.

Christopher Lee as Scaramanga

Lee's performance contains many of the elements which he brought to other dominating and destructive figures. The difference here is that he was now playing to a more general audience. There are echoes of Dracula, Lord Summerisle, Rasputin and Chung King in his performance. Scaramanga, like these other characters, is an extreme embodiment of evil. They could easily fall into caricature. To Lee's credit, that never happens.

His interpretation focuses on two critical aspect of Scaramanga's personality. The first is domination. Scaramanga does not kill primarily for money (although wealth is certainly important to him, given his lifestyle). He kills to express his dominance, his power. Scaramanga's ultimate goal is to use solar energy both as a weapon and a bargaining chip with the nations of the world. He kills Hai Fat as a means to getting his scientific resources. This aspect of domination is seen in the moment when Scaramanga, offering to show Bond the power of his solar energy, blows up Bond's plane. There is a playful smile on Scaramanga's face as he does so. The real issue is not taking away Bond's means of escape. Scaramanga is like a child with a new toy at Christmas. More than anything else, he is delighted with the prospect of having this kind of power. He enjoys doing it because it proves to him that he can do it.

Scaramanga is essentially alone. He has no interpersonal relationship with his servants, his henchmen or even his mistress. These people are all a means to an end in his game of domination. In his mind, they are not human beings in their own right. They are all pawns on his personal chessboard. The value they have for him is that they enable him to show off his dominance. Lee conveys this aspect of him perfectly. He looks down on them as though they were parts of a private collection of valuable objects. Their only function is to please him.

The second aspect that Lee conveys in the role is self-delusion. In all of Scaramanga's dialogue with Bond on the island, he wants to convey the idea of how sporting he is. He is fair. He plays by the rules. But these rules have all been distorted in his mind. As noted, he sees no difference between his killings and Bond's. He thinks of himself as something of an artist. The ultimate example of his artistry is the solar energy mechanism he has built. Yet he is more impressed with its destructive power than he is with any idea of solving the energy crisis. Lee conveys as much with his voice and facial expressions. He explains his plans in the tone that a museum guide might use. He is intrigued by what he does but he can explain it all in a matter-of-fact way, as if to say, "Oh, look. I just blew up your plane." Lee's uses a half-smile expression to suggest how perfectly normal Scaramanga thinks this is. He is content with all he has done and takes it for granted that others will have the same reaction. His eyes, however, convey an intensity that indicates a degree of madness.

There's a classic example of his self-delusion in the beginning of the duel scene on the beach. Scaramanga claims this will be a classic duel. They will stand back to back, walk off 20 paces, then turn and shoot. He insists this is all "fair play," the way gentlemen should act. Bond is prepared to go along with it (he has little choice). Yet Scaramanga cheats. Instead of walking the 20 paces, he runs off and hides himself. Even by his own rules, this is not playing fair. Lee does an admirable job of having Scaramanga say all this with a straight face and full conviction. He has in his own mind done this all appropriately. He is not taking unfair advantage. In his world, this is fairness. In his demented way, being fair means doing whatever is necessary to advance his cause. He is then supremely self-delusional.

It appears that Lee was concerned about being typecast throughout his career. Presumably that is why he didn't repeat his role as Dracula for eight years. He played a range of other characters even in Hammer films including two appearances as a pirate (*The Devil-Ship Pirates, The Pirates of Blood River*). Yet his greatest achievements were in playing intense, focused figures in some kind of moral conflict. While many of these were villains of one kind of another, they could also be heroes (Duc du Richleau, Sherlock Holmes). As mentioned, Scaramanga's character brings together traits and aspects of Lee's earlier roles both at Hammer and beyond. With *The Man with the Golden Gun,* he was finally able to display his talents to a wider cinema audience.

14

To the Devil a Daughter (1976)

To the Devil a Daughter was Hammer's last horror film (until its revival in the 21st century). It was also the next-to-last film released under the Hammer name (the last was a remake of the Alfred Hitchcock classic *The Lady Vanishes*). To put it bluntly, it is a terrible film. But it's worth discussing for two reasons. First, it is the end of Hammer's long and, for the most part, impressive run. Second, it contains one of Christopher Lee's most impressive performances. It is unfortunate that this occurs in such a weak film.

The Context of the Film

By 1975, Hammer's decline was past recovery. Noting the occult trend in horror (*Rosemary's Baby, The Exorcist*), they tried to adapt. They had some success with *Satanic Rites of Dracula,* but since that film could not find a major distributor in the U.S., its benefit to the company was minimal. Hammer, desperate, turned to the source of one of their best films: author Dennis Wheatley, whose *The Devil Rides Out* had been a superb example of an occult horror film. That film had the benefit of Hammer's original team which included Terence Fisher (director), Anthony Nelson-Keys (producer). Arthur Grant (cinematographer), Bernard Robinson (set designer) and James Bernard (composer). But by 1975, that team was no longer working at Hammer.

Lee had urged Hammer to consider filming the works of Dennis Wheatley well before they did *The Devil Rides Out*. Hammer adapted *The Devil Rides Out* and a science fiction–type story, *The Lost Continent* (1968), the latter based on Wheatley's *Uncharted Seas*. Wheatley, not surprisingly, was very pleased with *The Devil Rides Out* and so was more than willing to have Hammer film other books of his.

The impetus for *Daughter* was clearly the impact of 1973's *The Exorcist*.

However rather than adapt the occult theme to their Gothic tradition, as they had done with *The Devil Rides Out* and even *Satanic Rites of Dracula,* Hammer attempted to outdo *The Exorcist* in a striking portrayal of black magic and the demonic. The end result was a disaster, a film which is not only tasteless but appears to dabble in the very evil it portrays. Hammer here had gone back to their old practice of casting older American actors in the lead. In a part that cries out for Peter Cushing, Richard Widmark plays the lead. He portrays John Verney who, like Wheatley, is the author of occult thrillers. Widmark apparently was very unhappy with the production and threatened to leave to go back to the U.S. on several occasions. In any event, the real star of the film is Christopher Lee.

The Film

In Germany, a Roman Catholic service is in progress: Father Michael Rayner (Lee) is being excommunicated for heresy. He will create his own church, "The Children of the Lord," which worships the god Astaroth, who is pictured standing over an upside-down cross.

In London, American author John Verney (Widmark) is about to do a book signing arranged by his English agents, a married couple named David and Anna Fountain (Anthony Valentine, Honor Blackman). The book signing is not open to the general public but a very agitated man, Henry Beddows (Denholm Elliott), arrives insisting he has to talk with Verney. As we will learn as the convoluted script unfolds, Beddows and his wife Margaret (Izabella Telezynska) made a pact with Lee's demonic "church," the Children of the Lord, to have their daughter baptized to eventually be the bride of the demon Astaroth. Margaret has to die in childbirth for this to happen. Father Rayner presides over the birth. The ghost of Margaret warns Henry that he is to abide by this pact and he is given a curved medallion which is to remind him of all this. The medallion will erupt in flames if this is not all carried out.

Years later, the daughter, Catherine (Nastassja Kinski), dressed as a Roman Catholic nun but really a member of the Satanic Children of the Lord, arrives in London to fulfill her destiny. Terrified of all this, her father asks Verney to meet her at the airport and keep her with him so that the Satanists will not find her. At one point, Rayner phones Henry demanding to know her whereabouts. Henry initially resists but Rayner uses his black magic to turn Henry's phone into a serpent. Terrified, Henry reveals the girl's location. Father Rayner is supported by another couple, George and Evelyn De Grass (Michael Goodliffe. Eva Marie Meineke).

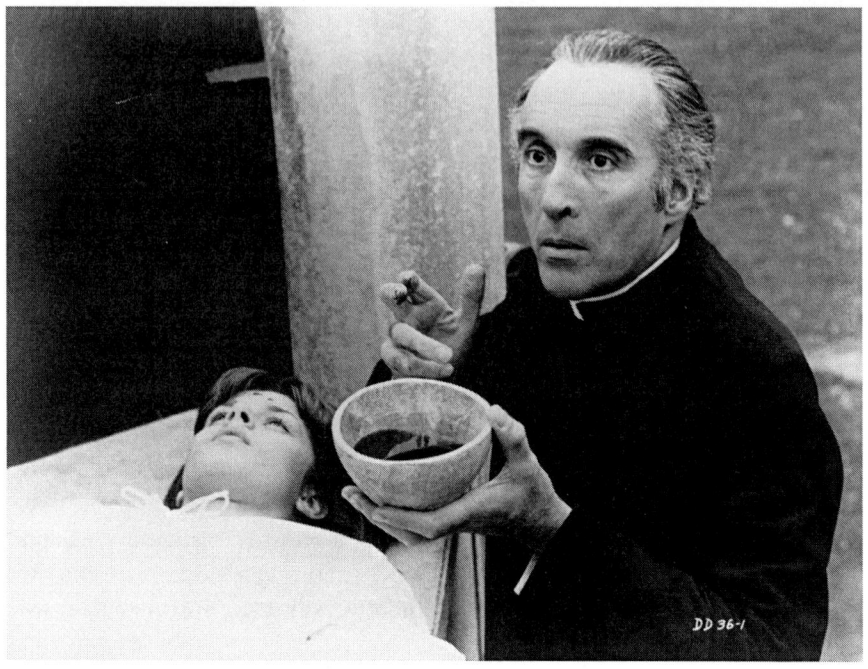

Catherine (Nastassja Kinski) is about to undergo a demonic baptism at the hands of the fallen priest, Father Rayner (Christopher Lee), in *To the Devil a Daughter* (1976).

Verney tries to make Catherine comfortable but the girl is tormented by a dream of a woman in labor whose legs are tied together. The woman dies giving birth. Verney tries to learn the truth about all this. He becomes convinced that Catherine is in the grip of a dangerous satanic cult. He finds Catherine in a seemingly hypnotic trance in the street and brings her back to his apartment. He asks David and Anna to stay with Catherine while he tries to learn more about the mysterious god Astaroth. Verney visits a Bishop friend (Derek Francis) who brings him into a restricted church library where he consults an ancient book about the mysterious god. He becomes convinced that Catherine is being groomed to be the mother of an incarnate form of the god. Catherine has a horrible dream of a blood-covered demonic fetus crawling into her vagina.

Catherine kills Anna with a knife and escapes. David insists on going with Verney to find Catherine. They visit her father, who has locked himself in a room and sits terrified inside a chalk-drawn circle (reminiscent of the protective circle in *The Devil Rides Out*). Henry, deeply agitated, tells Verney and David that the medallion he was initially given is now in a church. He also tells them where the cult is located. Verney has already determined that Catherine's final baptism into the cult will take place on All Hallow's Eve (Halloween). Verney and David find the medallion in the church as Henry indicated. David takes hold of the medallion and bursts into flames. Wind sweeps through the deserted church as Verney cries out to the demon, "Damn you!"

In preparation for the fatal consecration of Catherine, Father Rayner's ally Eveline drains out her own blood and, as a result, dies. Verney arrives at the estate where the cult is lodged but he is alone. The estate is guarded by Father Rayner's "disciples." Verney picks up a stone and strikes one of the disciples on the head. Verney is then able to make his way on to the estate. Next he sees Father Rayner sacrificing the baby whose tortured birth we witnessed earlier. A sacrificial altar has been prepared on the front lawn. Father Rayner makes a circle of blood around it. At this point, Verney confronts him. Rayner suggests that they cease this conflict: If Verney is willing to join them, he will receive the power and pleasure that supposedly attends the worshippers of Astaroth. Rayner goes so far as to offer Verney the sexual pleasure of Catherine herself. Rayner gives him a vision of Catherine disrobing and coming towards him completely naked.

Verney challenges Rayner, insisting that he will take Catherine back. He tells Rayner that he has read the Book of Astaroth. In a very smug manner, Rayner responds that, if that is so, then Verney should know that he will not be able to penetrate the circle of blood. Rayner adds that the estate is built over ground containing flint, which is the favored stone of their god. Verney answers that the stone he holds has the blood of one of Rayner's disciples on it. As a result, the demons are now angry with Rayner. Therefore, Verney argues, the demons will now protect him. With that, Verney steps into the circle of blood and throws the stone at Father Rayner and apparently kills him.

Verney rescues Catherine, who wipes the blood markings from her forehead. The film ends with a quote from Dennis Wheatley—who apparently was appalled by the production and swore he would not allow Hammer to film any more of his novels. He needn't have worried. This film was the death of Hammer Horror. Christopher Lee would not make another Hammer film until 2011 when he made a cameo appearance in *The Resident*.

Key Themes

To the Devil a Daughter is a film with enormous problems. To say that it is confusing is to put it mildly. It goes beyond exploitation in its depictions of horror and cruelty. To evaluate it, I will identify its central themes and then deal with the film's inability to adequately deal with those themes.

The basic concept of the occult in the film is important. Both Rayner and Catherine emphasize that their worship of Astaroth is intended to benefit humanity. In their minds, Astaroth will lead to a new beginning. Early in the film, Catherine says that contemporary youth seem lost, and that they need something to believe in. The bishop who participated in Rayner's excommunication tells Verney that Rayner's heresy was his belief in the "absolute capability of man." Oddly, the bishop calls human beings a "freak of evolution" who cannot survive without God. In this sense, Rayner's heresy was that he placed too much confidence in human nature. At the conclusion of the film, Rayner offers Verney the unique power and pleasure of Astaroth.

The closing quote of the film speaks of following the light and avoiding the darkness. Yet what is so important is that the forces of darkness present themselves as angels of light. In the New Testament, the apostle Paul speaks of the fact that Satan disguises himself as "an angel of light" (II Corinthians 11:14). In reality, those who fall into the occult, even into evil itself, are horribly deluded about what is the nature of good. In one of his most chilling statements, Joseph Goebbels, Hitler's Minister of Propaganda, allegedly said that whatever failings the Nazis had, the one indisputably good thing they had done was the extermination of the Jews! As Hammer's director Terence Fisher had said years earlier, "If evil were ugly, it wouldn't be a problem."

However a major problem with *To the Devil a Daughter* is that the cult "The Children of the Lord" never looks appealing. As commanding and fascinating as Father Rayner is, he is still ultimately a sinister figure. We see hardly any of the benefits of following this satanic cult. To the contrary, we see ghastly treatment of women, especially women in labor. Even by today's standards, a number of scenes are intensely objectionable. We see Rayner slit the throat of a baby. The nude scene of the underage Natassja Kinski is more embarrassing than erotic. We are left with the question, why would anyone want to be part of this group?

The fundamental problem of this occult film is its depiction of the occult. This has to go beyond invocations of a demonic figure and bloody deaths. Among many unanswered questions is, why did Catherine's parents get involved with this group in the first place? Catherine's mother dies at her birth. We see what we can only imagine is her ghost, who appears to threaten their husband because he failed to honor the commitment they made to the cult. Years later, when Catherine is to take her place as the presumed consort of Astaroth, her father reacts with fear. In his one phone conversation with Rayner, the telephone turns into a snake. What benefit did he ever think this would have? How did he and his wife ever come into contact with the infamous Father Rayner and what, if anything, did they hope to receive in return for their daughter?

There are several points the film could have explored at this point but fails to do so. First, there is the classic theme of the Devil's bargain. The serpent in the Garden of Eden offers Adam and Eve the opportunity to become like God. Satan tempts Jesus with everything from bread to "all the kingdoms of the world and their splendor" (Matthew 4:8). Faust sells his soul to the Devil in exchange for a period of total prosperity and pleasure. In Christopher Marlowe's famous version "The Tragedy of Dr. Faustus," Faust is offered nothing less than Helen of Troy. This would seem far more beguiling than the very young Catherine. This, by the way, has to be another objectionable point in the film. Nastassja Kinski was underage when she made this film. Seeing her in full frontal nudity hardly seems appropriate.

This film could have explored the fairy tale tradition of the threatened princess. This would apply especially to Sleeping Beauty, Beauty (of "Beauty and the Beast") and Rapunzel. Each of these young women have been victimized by decisions others have made for them. Yet in each case, their parents were trapped by a good intention. Sleeping Beauty's parents certainly did not want to invite Maleficent to her party. Other parents made rash promises out of a need for money or shelter.

None of this is addressed in Catherine's case. Her father has made a pact with the Devil, but why? This also raises the question of Catherine's own choices. Beauty moves in with the Beast to free her father. Does Catherine have any choices or is she just a pawn of Father Rayner? If she had no capacity to choose, we need to ask *why*. Has she been nothing but a pawn her whole life? She apparently has seen her father at odd times while she was growing up in Germany. Did she never have any idea of her circumstances or, more to the point, her demonic fate? If Catherine has no choice at all, it is hard to see her as a victim. The various fairy tale princesses all have clear desires of their own. They may be forcibly restricted in a castle or a tower but invariably they want to break free from the witch, beast or whatever holds them captive. If Catherine is nothing more than a cipher, then it is hard to be concerned about her.

The final key theme here and the one that is central to Christopher Lee's films is the struggle between good and evil. One of the concerns that I have discussed in the post-modern horror film beginning with *Rosemary's Baby* is the focus on the triumph of evil. In *The Exorcist,* the demon is finally cast out but there is hardly a sense of good overcoming evil since both priests involved in the exorcism die. One of the few strengths of *To the Devil a Daugh-*

ter is the fact that—in the style of older Hammer films—good, in the form of John Verney, does defeat the Satanist Father Rayner and rescue Catherine. Yet this positive feature is compromised by the strange way it is shown in the film.

John Verney is out of his league in his encounter with "The Children of the Lord." He is no Van Helsing, Duc de Richleau or Father Sandor. The man and wife he calls on to help him die horrible deaths. His help for Catherine's father is limited to his providing Catherine with shelter. He appears to be no match for the forces surrounding Catherine and he underestimates the evil possessing her. He then is totally unprepared for Catherine's murdering Anna Fountain. Once he has visited the bishop and has actually read the Book of Astaroth, why does he not ask the bishop for help? Going alone to the Satanists' domain seems risky, if not foolish. He watches helplessly as a baby's throat is cut. Why isn't he accompanied by the priests who could call down God's wrath on Rayner? For that matter, why aren't the police consulted? How is Verney going to account for the dead bodies of Anna and David Fountain?

Granted that good is going to finally win out here, its victory appears perplexing. Verney's sole weapon against Rayner is a bloodied stone which he uses to knock out (or kill?) one of Rayner's guards. Verney claims that Rayner has angered the demons because of his disciple's death. Why is this? Second, Verney says that the demons will protect him and they will bring about the destruction of Rayner. This picks up a dubious theme from Hammer's earlier *The Kiss of the Vampire* where vampires are killed by demonic bats conjured up by the film's Van Helsing–like professor. (Apparently this ending was conceived for *The Brides of Dracula* but was rejected by both star Peter Cushing and director Terence Fisher.) However, rather than this being a clear case of good overcoming evil, it is more the idea of evil overcoming itself. This is, at best, a dubious take on the theme.

Verney defeats Rayner by throwing the rock at him. Apparently the rock kills him. Why is this? At this stage, very little is clear. The film supposedly was to end with Rayner being struck by lightning but this was dropped because it seemed to be a repeat of Dracula's death in the earlier *Scars of Dracula*.

This is a very sad end to Hammer's great tradition. Yet in spite of all these drawbacks, the film offers an outstanding Christopher Lee performances.

Christopher Lee as Father Rayner

Lee portrays Father Rayner as the very embodiment of evil. This is especially effective given the fact that Lee's performance is very restrained. He conveys the sense of a person simply going about his regular duties. In this case, his duty is to serve the demonic figure Astaroth. At the same time, Lee registers a perverse delight in the evil which he serves. His face often betrays a smirk rather than a fully malicious smile. His delight in what he does affords him satisfaction but he continually underplays the pleasure it gives him. This comes across in two pivotal scenes. The first is his telephone call to Catherine's father Henry, when he is able to take hold of a few ropes and turn Henry's phone into a snake. The look in Lee's eyes and the tone of his voice indicates that he enjoys having this power over Henry. The second involves his final encounter with Verney. He raises the question, again with a slight smirk, as to why they have to be enemies. He invokes the promise of power and then offers the nude Catherine. There is a sense of self-satisfaction as he does this. He delights in the fact that, in his mind, he has the upper hand. There are no outbursts here, no sharply spoken threats. Everything is low-key.

One remarkable aspect to Lee's performance is the way he speaks of the women who submit to death as a way of advancing the cause of Astaroth. This includes Catherine's mother as well as the later birth scene (which Catherine identifies with even in Verney's apartment). It also includes Eveline, who commits suicide by lying on a bed, putting a needle into her arm and then pumping out her blood until she dies. Rayner speaks of each of them with a sense of gratitude. He appreciates their sacrifice. In his distorted mind, they have advanced the cause of a great god the way we might speak of a police officer or firefighter who gave their lives in the line of duty. As bizarre as this is, Lee pulls it off with conviction. Rayner really is grateful for their "sacrifice."

Lee portrays Rayner as a totally unsympathetic figure. Whenever he speaks of the benefits of his cult, we are invariably confronted with its cruelty and violence. Lee's portrayal is unsparing. His Father Rayner is even more cold-blooded than Count Dracula, Rasputin and Lord Summerisle. Yet he remains fascinating. He holds our interest. We watch him the way we would view a snake. For all the failures of this film, it has the distinction of giving us one of Lee's finest performances.

The Lord of the Rings

The Fellowship of the Ring (2001),
The Two Towers (2002), *The Return of the King* (2003),
The Hobbit: An Unexpected Journey (2013),
The Battle of Five Armies (2014)

The Context of the Films

Toward the end of his career, Christopher Lee had secondary but important roles in two of the biggest fantasy film franchises in history, *The Lord of the Rings* and *Star Wars*. By this point in his career, he had made a number of cameo appearances in fantasy films which were essentially a form of tribute from younger directors who had grown up watching his films. In addition to Peter Jackson's *Lord of the Rings* and George Lucas' *Star Wars*, there were *Sleepy Hollow* (1999), *Charlie and the Chocolate Factory* (2005), *The Corpse Bride* (2005) *Dark Shadows* (2012), all directed by Tim Burton, plus *Gremlins 2: The New Batch* (1990), directed by Joe Dante, and *Hugo* (2011), directed by Martin Scorsese.

By far the most elaborate films Lee had ever appeared in was the three-part *Lord of the Rings*. (His death in the third installment *Return of the King*, did not include his death in the theatrical version but the scene was included in the expanded version on video.) Lee was a huge fan of J.R.R. Tolkien's fantasy masterpiece and had read it once a year ever since the first volume was published in England in 1954. The director Peter Jackson had been a fan of Lee's since childhood, owning a 16mm print of *Dracula, Prince of Darkness*. Lee originally wanted to play Gandalf in the epic, but it was felt that he was too old and he was given the part of the wizard, Sarurman the White.

The Lord of the Rings had an eventful and intriguing history. J.R.R. Tolkien, a professor of philology (language) at Oxford University, and his friend C.S. Lewis in effect started an informal gathering of scholars and writers which became known as the Inklings. They would meet weekly in Lewis' rooms or in a local pub, The Eagle and the Child. Among others present at these gatherings were author Charles Williams (*All Hallows Eve, Descent into Hell, War in Heaven*) and Owen Barfield, who shared Tolkien's interest in language. This group met off and on for almost 30 years.

What drew them together was a love of mythology and fantasy. Several of them, including Lewis and Tolkien, were deeply religious (Tolkien led a previously atheistic Lewis to Christian faith). In the academic environment of Oxford in this period, neither myth nor religion was taken very seriously, but the Inklings were very serious about both. Their interest in mythology embraced both Classic Greek and Norse literature. In his famous essay "On Fairy-Stories," Tolkien laid out a contemporary understanding of myth. For Tolkien, "Fairy" referred to a whole realm of fantasy and the imagination. It was in effect an alternate universe. Yet it was a world which in terms of the imagination was very real, a world containing truths that could illuminate our physical, historical world. Tolkien was not conceiving of gods and goddesses descending directly into human history as was the case in the ancient myths. Instead he imagined a parallel world of the imagination which offered its own light and truth. For both Lewis and Tolkien, the one place where the two worlds converged was in the incarnation of Jesus Christ, the Word made flesh (Gospel of John 1:1). Lewis contributed an essay on Christian faith as an example of myth becoming fact.

Lamenting the lack of fantasy and imagination in the modern world, the Inklings began writing their own stories. They read passages to each other and critiqued their work. These exchanges were the origin of Middle-earth, featured fully-formed in *The Hobbit* and *The Lord of the Rings*. Middle-earth precedes our Earth and its history. We are not part of it but we can learn from it. Middle-earth lays the foundation for Lewis' Narnia (which Tolkien was not pleased with), Harry Potter's parallel world of magic and *Star Wars'* "galaxy far, far away." Many of Lee's Hammer films take place in an essentially parallel fantasy world. For example, there is no clearly identifiable location in Hammer's *Dracula*.

The Lord of the Rings was initially published in three hardcover volumes in England in the mid–1950s: *The Fellowship of the Ring, The Two Towers* and *The Return of the King*. Almost immediately, its cinematic possibilities were noted. One of the first figures in Hollywood to discuss their filming was Forrest J Ackerman, just at the time he was launching his magazine *Famous Monsters of Filmland* which influenced many of the same filmmakers who grewn up watching Lee's films (including Peter Jackson). Tolkien was far from happy with the script and the project never developed.

Tolkien died in 1973 without ever seeing a film version of his literary masterpiece. Four years later, Julius Bass and Arthur Rankin, Jr., who were known for the animated Christmas specials *Frosty the Snow Man* and *Rudolph the Red Nosed Reindeer,* produced an animated version of *The Hobbit.* This was followed the next year by an animated version of *The Lord of the Rings.* Neither film was especially well-received.

In 1977, film fantasy got a huge boost from the release of *Star Wars* which included Lee's frequent co-star Peter Cushing in the cast. This was followed by a wave of big-budget fantasy films, many of them drawing on familiar comic book heroes such as Superman, Batman and Spider-Man. This trend culminated in an elaborate live-action version of Tolkien's great work. *The Fellowship of the Ring* was released in 2001 followed by *The Two Towers* and *The Return of the King* and three prequels based on the earlier *The Hobbit.*

The Films

The Lord of the Rings is a literary epic. Peter Jackson's film version is also an epic in its own right. Including the extended versions, the three part film runs over ten hours. This invites comparison to another epic about a ring of power, Richard Wagner's four-part opera masterwork *The Ring of the Nibelungs.* Tolkien's work, like Wagner's, includes a host of characters, sub-plots and massive action.

In an ancient age before history as we know it began, there existed Middle-earth. It is populated by elves, dwarfs, dragons, wizards, tree-like characters known as Ents, humans and, most central to Tolkien's narrative, hobbits. Hobbits are small human-like figures with hairy feet. A hobbit named Bilbo Baggins finds a ring of power with which one could rule all of Middle-earth. The ring also comes with dark, destructive consequences even for the one who wears it. A figure named Smeagol had possessed the ring earlier, calling it his "precious." It drained him physically and mentally. He is now known as Gollum and longs for the ring.

Bilbo Baggins gives the ring to his nephew Frodo, who sets out to return it to its original source on Mount Doom and destroy it, thereby freeing Middle-earth from its corrupting power. Frodo is aided by his hobbit friends Samwise Gamgee, Merry and Pippin. The quest includes Aragorn, a king in exile; Gimli, a dwarf warrior; Legalos, an elf, among other humans and elves. Guiding Frodo is the wizard Gandalf the Grey. Arrayed against Frodo and his supporters is the former wizard friend of Gandalf, Saruman the White (played by Lee). In the film, he has allied himself with the evil lord Sauron, who desires the ring to gain control of all of Middle-earth. After many adventures and the temptations of the ring itself, Frodo with the aid of Samwise destroys the ring by hurling it into the fire of Mount Doom.

Each of the films in the trilogy was well-received with the last, *The Return of the King,* winning the Oscar for Best Picture. Yet the films, of necessity, take a number of liberties with the original Tolkien story. Several of these relate to Lee's evil wizard Saruman. The films capture the essential spirit of the novels, which Tolkien insisted were not allegories, spiritual or philosophical. In this sense, Tolkien was distancing himself from the great allegories of the English language such as *The Faerie Queen* (1595) by Edmund Spencer and *The Pilgrim's Progress* (1688) by John Bunyan. In those works which clearly influenced Tolkien with their heroes, dragons, fairies and knights, each figure stands for

Christopher Lee as Saruman the White of the *Lord of the Rings* saga.

some trait or even identifiable real-life character. In Spencer's classic, the Fairy Queen represents Queen Elizabeth I. The Red Cross Knight stands for Holiness. Bunyan is even more direct: His hero, also on a quest, is simply "Christian." Other characters are equally defined by their names, such as Mr. Worldly Wiseman. C.S. Lewis followed the same pattern in his *Chronicles of Narnia* series in which the great lion Aslan is clearly a symbol of Christ. Despite Tolkien's protestations, there is an element of Christ in his king, Aragorn, who is described in Biblical terms in the third novel as "ancient of days," a quote from the Book of Daniel 7:9.

These points are very germane to anyone seeking to film Tolkien's epic. The writers and directors have to decide not only what to cut or include from the extensive narrative but in a larger sense decide what kind of story they intend to film. On the most superficial level, *The Lord of the Rings* could be seen purely as an adventure story. There are good characters facing off against evil ones with a healthy dose of battles, monsters and romance. Yet such a reading of Tolkien scarcely does justice to his great trilogy. Jackson and his collaborators had to face the question: If there is a larger meaning to Tolkien's epic, what is it and how can it be presented on screen? In spite of Tolkien rejecting the idea that his work is an allegory, it parallels much of the Biblical narrative. There is an original fall from a good creation into evil. There is a figure of pure evil and an anointed king who opposes him. There is a final redemption. Frodo's journey with its dangers and temptations certainly echoes those of Christian in *The Pilgrim's Progress*.

Jackson and his collaborators did not want to simply film an adventurous fantasy and let it go at that. However, it is in giving a rationale to the multi-faceted story that the film is at its weakest. Sam gives an essential interpretation of the events at the end of *The Two Towers* when he tells Frodo that "stories really matter" (obviously including this one). There is darkness and danger but the darkness must pass. The sunshine at the end will be brighter and clearer. Hope doesn't turn back. We have to hold on to something. There's some good in this world and it's worth fighting for. Unfortunately, these sentiments have all the depth of a greeting card.

Tolkien attempted to say more than this. To give an example: Sam states that hope doesn't turn back. Tolkien commenting on his work in his letters said that he was concerned with the idea that hope has no guarantees (Tolkien, *Letters,* p. 237). Despite a surface similarity to these two statements, there is a difference. The film is saying that hope doesn't "turn back," it keeps on. It will win out because the darkness must pass into the sunshine. Tolkien's own statement goes further. For him, hope must endure with no assurance that it will prevail or endure. The film offers a rosy optimism that is not in Tolkien's original work. The real issues for Tolkien are the misuse of power, the danger of impatience and the validation of humility.

Christopher Lee as Saruman

The character of Saruman the White shows the differences between the films and Tolkien's original novels. When we first meet Saruman in the first film, he is shown to be an old friend of Gandalf's. He is initially cordial but soon reveals that he is now in league with the dark lord Sauron. He and Gandalf have a major battle, and Gandalf barely escapes.

Throughout the films, Saruman is an evil figure serving Sauron. In the extended version of *The Return of the King*, he is given an opportunity to repent by revealing Sauron's plans to Gandalf and his allies. When he refuses, he is killed by one of his own followers. Lee infuses the character with his dominating voice and presence. He intones dark threats like "There will be no dawn for man." Yet in the final analysis, Saruman is presented in the films as a "bad guy," a classic villain. His devotion to Sauron is never fully explained except for the point that he wants to have a place of power and privilege once Sauron has dominated all of Middle-earth.

In Tolkien's view, there is much more to Saruman. He is neither inherently evil nor is he simply a disciple of Sauron. Initially he is inclined to "good ends" but he succumbs to impatience. Tolkien appears to be saying that it is not enough to desire the good. There seems to be a sense in which one must wait for it. The temptation that leads to Saruman's downfall is his desire to misuse power in order to gain his ends. Tolkien sees him as persuasive but not hypnotic (*Letters*, p. 276–77). When he seeks to dominate others, even in a good cause, he has given in to the power of evil (*Letters* p. 237).

In the novels, Saruman is not a servant of Sauron. Saruman desires the ring for himself so in this sense he is a rival to Sauron. The paradox of his character in the films is that he is actually given a more prominent role in the story. Yet in a more significant sense, his role is diminished. For Tolkien, Saruman illustrates the whole dilemma of the ring. The ring is complete power, "one ring to rule them all." It is this dominating pursuit of power, even when one can claim that the power will be used in a good cause, which leads to corruption. The problem of impatience is that it forces one's hand. It makes a person claim to do more, to know more, than they actually do. In Tolkien's words, it leads to the desire to make one's will effective by any means. This is the supreme temptation of the ring even for Frodo, to have the power to carry out whatever desire he has.

It is not only the goal of achieving one's desire that is intoxicating. It is the process that leads to that goal. This in turn creates the very real danger of seeking unrestrained power. That effort is in itself exhilarating. Against this stands the essential humility of Frodo and the other hobbits, especially Sam. In carrying the terrible burden of the ring, they seek no special reward, no exalted status. They are doing what must be done. This in effect is how Gandalf initially presents the mission of returning the ring to Mount Doom. The ring must be finally and completely destroyed. It must be eliminated if there is to be any hope for Middle-earth. Hope is not guaranteed. The ring in itself represents the full corruption of power. It is therefore evil. However, contrary to Sam's positive prediction, there is no guarantee of success. Saruman's resources at any given moment seem no less powerful than Gandalf's.

Essentially, Saruman's character is much more nuanced in the original books that it is in the films. This could be said about the films as a whole. Obviously characters and events had to be reshaped from the original books. This is inevitable. Movies are a different medium than literature. Yet, unfortunately, many of the more critical themes of the books seem to have been lost in the transition from the written page to film. This is especially the case with the character of Saruman. As written in the screenplay, the character is two-dimensional at best. He finally appears to be little more than a conventional villain. Granted, Lee plays him very effectively. That is no surprise. The unfortunate thing is that Lee's performance could have been much more. If Saruman's impatience for the good, and his succumbing to his own persuasive abilities, could have been shown more fully, the character could have been closer to Tolkien's original conception. One can only imagine what he could have done if the tragedy of Saruman had been fleshed out.

Filming a massive work like *The Lord of the Rings* is a daunting challenge. We should appreciate Jackson's films for being as good as they are, even *with* their flaws. Lee certainly is an imposing wizard. Yet more of his "fall," in Tolkien's words, could have been explored even in his brief appearances in *The Hobbit*. By the time we get to *The Battle of the Five Armies,* we seem just to be watching an exciting fantasy adventure.

Lee's role as Saruman put him in front of a worldwide audience and enabled him to appear in an Oscar-winning Best Picture. At least in the expanded version.

16

Star Wars

Episode II—Attack of the Clones (2002),
Episode III—Revenge of the Sith (2005)

The Context of the Films

George Lucas' original *Star Wars* (1977) changed our culture. This is
no light statement but it is one that can certainly be defended. *Star Wars* is
not really science fiction since there are no references to Earth in it at all.
Invariably science fiction deals with a theme that relates to Earth either in
the present or the future. *Star Wars* takes place "long ago in a galaxy far, far
away." The film in reality is an epic fantasy. In short, it is a myth. We are
dealing here with the alternate universe which Tolkien outlined in his concept of "faerie." Its mystical character is further brought out by the fact that
Joseph Campbell, author of *The Hero with a Thousand Faces* and the multi-
volume *The Masks of God,* was a resource for the film. Campbell, who taught
myth at Columbia University, was perhaps the leading scholar in the United
States on the subject of mythology. In a public broadcasting interview with
Bill Moyers, he talked about *Star Wars* and how it reveals the essential mythical journey of the hero. Without *Star Wars,* it is hard to imagine the continuing popularity of everything from Harry Potter to comic book film
franchises to the growing curriculum of courses in mythology on university
campuses.

Fantasy, to say nothing of myth, had always been regarded as a secondary
film genre at best. The acknowledged initial science fiction masterpiece
Metropolis (1926), directed by Fritz Lang, failed at the box office upon its initial release and was heavily edited to make it more appealing. It has only
recently been restored to its original length. Its futuristic sky scenes show up
in several of the *Star Wars* films. In general, however, outer space was usually
seen only in B movies and serials. For that matter, the scrolling text at the
beginning of each *Star Wars* episode is taken from the space fantasy serials

Flash Gordon and *Buck Rogers*. Reportedly, Lucas wanted originally to re-film *Flash Gordon* but he couldn't afford to pay for the rights.

I remember coming into a theater in Philadelphia just as the original *Star Wars* was beginning. Seeing the rolling credits with John Williams' pulsating orchestral score, all I could think of was the serial *Flash Gordon Conquers the Universe* which had the same format (and its musical score was the exciting climax of Franz Liszt's *Les Preludes*). The Flash Gordon movie serials had been shown many times on independent television stations in the 1950s and '60s. They had been seen multiple times not only by Lucas but by a whole generation of fantasy "geeks" (including myself).

Prior to *Star Wars*, serious fantasy and science fiction films had been few and far between. As beloved as some of these films are now, like *The Day the Earth Stood Still*, *The Blob* and even low-grade efforts like *Invasion of the Saucer Men*, they were hardly taken seriously in their own time. Even films of classic myth like *Jason and the Argonauts* were deemed appropriate primarily for juvenile audiences. (At a recent Oscar night, Tom Hanks, introducing a long overdue special Academy Award for Ray Harryhausen, confessed that his favorite film was *Jason and the Argonauts*.) Major film efforts like *Things to Come* (1936), *The War of the Worlds* (1953), *Forbidden Planet* (1956), *The Time Machine* (1960), *Planet of the Apes* (1968) and *2001: A Space Odyssey* (1968) were exceptions. Even so, as mentioned above, *Star Wars* did not fit a standard science fiction format. Lucas drew on multiple film sources including Akira Kurosawa's *The Hidden Fortress* (1958) and John Ford's *The Searchers* (1956).

Another source for Lucas, along with other directors of his generation such as Stephen Spielberg, Tim Burton, Joe Dante, Martin Scorsese and Peter Jackson, were England's Hammer Films. As I noted in the discussion of Tolkien, the Hammer films seemed to be set in some form of the "land of faerie." It is therefore no accident that Hammer's two main stars Peter Cushing and Christopher Lee show up in the *Star Wars* franchise. As if the reference to Hammer is not plain enough, Lee's character is Count Dooku, complete with a black cape. For that matter, Darth Vader's heavy breathing seems to come from the underappreciated *Frankenstein and the Monster from Hell* (1972) in which David Prowse as the monster also breathes heavily. Prowse portrays Darth Vader in *Star Wars* (though the voice of course is James Earl Jones).

Lee appears as Count Dooku in *Attack of the Clones* and *Revenge of the Sith*. He also voices the character in the animated *The Clone Wars*. The two live-action films are listed as episodes two and three in the saga but they were filmed as prequels to the first trilogy which now became known as *A New*

Hope, The Empire Strikes Back and *Return of the Jedi.* The full scope of these films is beyond the focus of the present work. I will look at the films from the standpoint of Lee's character Count Dooku.

The Films

As *Attack of the Clones* begins, the young Anakin Skywalker (Hayden Christensen) is a Jedi knight under the apprenticeship of Obi-Wan Kenobi (Ewan McGregor). The Jedi knights are a monastic group who have been taught to use "the force." The force basically unites all things. It appears to be a spiritual entity which gives enormous power. It also has a "dark side" which can be highly destructive. The Galactic Republic is threatened by a group that wishes to secede and, by implication, replace the democratic Republic with an authoritarian empire.

Star Wars presents us with a galaxy "far, far away" or, in Tolkien's terms, an alternate world. The Jedi knights are the peacekeepers of the Republic. Anakin and Obi-Wan have to care for Padmé Amidala (Natalie Portman), a former queen who now represents her planet as a senator. After an attempt is made on her life, she is placed under the protection of Anakin. Obi-Wan hunts for bounty hunter Jango Fett (Temuera Morrison), who allegedly was the would-be assassin.

Anakin and Obi-Wan learn of a conspiracy to overthrow the Republic. Behind this is a sinister group known as the Siths who have given themselves over to the dark side of the force. Their leader, former Jedi knight Count Dooku (Lee), is preparing an army to overpower the Jedis and destroy the Republic. Faced with this threat. the Senate, the governing body of the Republic, gives the chancellor, Palpatine (Ian McDiarmid), emergency powers. The chancellor secretly is also a Sith Lord whose ultimate desire is to destroy the Republic and establish himself as a dictator. His apprentice and loyal follower is Count

Christopher Lee played Count Dooku in Episodes 2 and 3 of the *Star Wars* saga.

Dooku. Jango Fett is to be the prototype whose body will be copied to create an army which eventually will be used to overthrow the Republic.

In the midst of this turmoil, Anakin faces the first of two personal crises. In one of the weakest moments in the film, he begins to fall in love with Padmé, whom he first met years ago and now is charged to protect. As a Jedi knight he is required to remain single, but the more time he spends with Padmé, the harder he finds it to resist her. This leads to some very hackneyed dialogue on the part of Lucas and his co-writer Jonathan Hales. Anakin to Padmé: "From the moment I first met you all those years ago, not a moment has gone by that I haven't thought of you…. You are in my very soul, tormenting me." This excessive heart-throb emoting unfortunately seems to invite a Groucho Marx–type response like, "Ever since I met you, I've swept you off my feet." Sadly, Anakin's relationship with Padmé is doomed by more than his soap opera expressions of love. They secretly marry but she dies giving birth to twins who will become Luke Skywalker and Princess Leia in the original *Star Wars,* which Lucas would retitle *A New Hope.*

Anakin's second crisis comes when his mother is kidnapped and killed on her home planet of Tatooine. Anakin is not satisfied simply to take revenge on those who kidnapped her but proceeds to kill their entire tribe. We are being prepared here for Anakin's turning to the dark side, which will culminate at the end of Episode III with his becoming Darth Vader. Before that happens however, both Anakin and Obi-Wan must confront Count Dooku, a former Jedi knight who has turned to the dark side and is preparing an army to overthrow the Republic. Count Dooku's goal is to help the scheming chancellor become dictator of the Galactic Empire.

Christopher Lee as Count Dooku

The real villain of *Attack of the Clones* and *Revenge of the Sith* is the devious Chancellor Palpatine, who will become the emperor of the soon-to-be-conquered Republic. The face of the separatist movement seeking to overthrow the Republic is Lee's Count Dooku. The title and, of course, the black cape are a homage to Lee's many portrayals of another count, Count Dracula. Lee here gives another masterful performance of an evil leader. He brings a malicious smile to his undertakings, reminiscent of his Lord Summerisle. As he had demonstrated in so many roles from Dracula to Saruman, he is a commanding presence issuing orders and defying anyone to oppose him.

One of his most memorable *Attack of the Clones* scenes is his light-saber duel with the master Jedi Yoda (voice of Frank Oz). Although much of the fight is obviously computerized, Lee's facial expressions reveal the intensity of his character. This duel and the one that leads to Dooku's death in *Revenge of the Sith* have a swashbuckling character more reminiscent of *The Three Musketeers* (in which Lee played the villainous Rochefort in the 1974 film and its sequel, 1989's *The Return of the Musketeers*) than of Lee's fantasy films.

In the duel at the beginning of *Revenge of the Sith* where Dooku is fighting with Obi-Wan and Anakin, Lucas gives Dooku the foreshadowing line spoken to Anakin, "I sense your fear." The same line will be said to Luke at the climax of *Return of the Jedi.* When Dooku is disarmed, Palpatine tells Anakin to kill him. There is stark fear in Dooku's face just before the light saber cuts off his life. (The character returned in the animated *The Clone Wars* with Lee furnishing the voice of Dooku.)

Lee is not a lead character either in *Star Wars* or *Lord of the Rings.* He is however a key figure in both. Both are evil presences with streaks of cruelty and goals of domination. Many of Lee's later roles are cameo appearances, especially in films directed by Tim Burton. He briefly reprised his role of Saruman in two of Peter Jackson's *Hobbit* films, *An Unexpected Journey* and *The Battle of the Five Armies.* He also made a brief appearance in Hammer's *The Resident* (2011). Yet in many ways his appearances in the *Lord of the Rings* and *Star Wars* series represent the culmination of a career in fantasy films where he was, more often than not, a villainous figure. At the same time, he invited sympathy from viewers. There was something tragic about his characters, from the Creature to Count Dooku. Lee could also portray strong characters representing goodness and light, from Sherlock Holmes to the Duc de Richleau. For those of us who began watching him in the Hammer Horrors in darkened theaters in the 1950s and continue to see him on home video screens well into the 21st century, Sir Christopher Lee remains a commanding and impressive film presence.

Lee often portrayed evil figures but in his films, evil was never finally victorious. The conflict between good and evil runs throughout his career. Yet in Lee's cinematic world, good invariably triumphed over evil. This is no small statement in a world where evil too often seems to be the stronger force. To quote from the Biblical text which Lee read at Peter Cushing's funeral, "The light shines in the darkness and the darkness did not overcome it" (John 1:5).

Filmography

The Curse of Frankenstein (1957) Hammer Films

Directed by Terence Fisher; Screenplay: Jimmy Sangster; From the novel by Mary Shelley; Photographer: Jack Asher; Art Director: Ted Marshall; Editor: James Needs; Music: James Bernard; Executive Producer: Michael Carreras; Associate Producer: Anthony Nelson-Keys; Producer: Anthony Hinds

Stars: Peter Cushing, Christopher Lee, Hazel Court, Robert Urquhart, Valerie Gaunt

Dracula (aka **Horror of Dracula**) (1958) Hammer Films

Directed by Terence Fisher; Screenplay: Jimmy Sangster; From the novel by Bram Stoker; Art Director: Bernard Robinson; Editors: James Needs and Bill Lenny; Music: James Bernard; Produced by Anthony Hinds

Stars: Peter Cushing, Christopher Lee, Michael Gough, Melissa Stribling, Carol Marsh, Olga Dickie, John Van Eyssen, Valerie Gaunt, Miles Malleson

The Hound of the Baskervilles (1959) Hammer Films

Directed by Terence Fisher; Screenplay: Peter Bryan; From the novel by Sir Arthur Conan Doyle; Photographer: Jack Asher; Art Director: Bernard Robinson; Editor: James Needs; Music: James Bernard; Executive Producer: Michael Carreras; Associate Producer: Anthony Nelson-Keys; Produced by Anthony Hinds

Stars: Peter Cushing, Andre Morell, Christopher Lee, Marla Landi, Ewen Solon, Francis De Wolff, Miles Malleson, David Oxley, John Le Mesurier

The Mummy (1959) Hammer Films

Directed by Terence Fisher; Screenplay: Jimmy Sangster; Based on Universal's films *The Mummy* (1932), *The Mummy's Hand* (1940), *The Mummy's Tomb* (1942), *The Mummy's Ghost* and *The Mummy's Curse* (both 1944); Photographer: Jack Asher; Art Director: Bernard Robinson; Editors: James Needs and Alfred Cox; Music: Frank Reizenstein; Associate Producer: Anthony Nelson-Keys; Produced by Michael Carreras

Stars: Peter Cushing, Christopher Lee, Yvonne Furneaux, Felix Aylmer, Eddie Byrne, Raymond Huntley, George Pastell

Taste of Fear (aka **Scream of Fear**) (1961) Hammer Films

Directed by Seth Holt; Produced by Jimmy Sangster and Michael Carreras; Screenplay: Jimmy Sangster; Music: Clifton Parker; Photographer: Douglas Slocombe; Editor: Eric Boyd-Perkins

Stars: Susan Strasberg, Ronald Lewis, Ann Todd, Christopher Lee

The Terror of the Tongs (1961) Hammer Films

Directed by Anthony Bushell; Executive Producer: Michael Carreras; Associate Producer: Anthony Nelson-Keys; Screenplay: Jimmy Sangster; Music: James Bernard; Photographer: Arthur Grant; Editor: Eric Boyd-Perkins

Stars: Christopher Lee, Yvonne Monlaur, Geoffrey Toone, Marne Maitland

Sherlock Holmes and the Deadly Necklace (1962)

Directed by Terence Fisher and Frank Witherstein; Screenplay: Curt Siodmak; Based on "The Valley of Fear" by Sir Arthur Conan Doyle; Produced by Arthur Brauner; Photographer: Richard Angst

Stars: Christopher Lee, Thorley Walters, Senta Berger, Hans Sohnker; Hans Neilsen

Rasputin the Mad Monk (1966) Hammer Films-Seven Arts

Directed by Don Sharp; Produced by Anthony Nelson-Keys; Screenplay: Anthony Hinds; Music: Don Banks; Photographer: Michael Reed; Editor: Roy Hyde

Stars: Christopher Lee, Barbara Shelley, Francis Matthews, Richard Pasco, Suzan Farmer

Dracula, Prince of Darkness (1966) Hammer Films-Seven Arts

Directed by Terence Fisher; Screenplay: John Sansom; From an idea by John Elder (Anthony Hinds); Photographer: Michael Reed; Production Designer: Bernard Robinson; Art Director: Don Mingaye; Editors: James Needs and Chris Barnes; Music: James Bernard; Produced by Anthony Nelson-Keys

Stars: Christopher Lee, Barbara Shelley, Andrew Keir, Francis Matthews, Suzan Farmer, Charles Tingwell, Thorley Walters

The Devil Rides Out (aka **The Devil's Bride**) (1968) Hammer Films

Directed by Terence Fisher; Screenplay: Richard Matheson; From the novel by Dennis Wheatley; Photographer: Arthur Grant; Art Director: Bernard Robinson; Editors: James Needs and Spencer Reeves; Music: James Bernard; Produced by Anthony Nelson-Keys

Stars: Christopher Lee, Charles Gray, Nike Arrighi, Leon Greene, Patrick Mower

The Private Life of Sherlock Holmes (1970) Mirisch Production Company-United Artists

Produced and Directed by Billy Wilder; Screenplay: Billy Wilder and I.A.L. Diamond; Set Designer: Alexander Trauner

Stars: Robert Stephens, Colin Blakely, Irene Handl, Stanley Holloway, Christopher Lee, Genevieve Page

I Monster (1971) Amicus Productions

Directed by Stephen Weeks; Produced by John Dark, Max Rosenberg and Milton Subotsky; Screenplay: Milton Subotsky; Based on *The Strange Case of Dr. Jekyll and Mr. Hyde* by Robert Louis Stevenson; Music: Carl Davis

Stars: Christopher Lee, Peter Cushing, Mike Raven, Richard Hurndall, George Merritt, Kenneth J. Warren, Susan Jameson

Horror Express (1972)

Directed by Eugenio Martin; Produced by Bernard Gordon and Gregorio Sacristan; Screenplay: Arnaud d'Usseau and Julian Zimet; Music: John Cacavas; Editor: Robert C. Dearberg

Stars: Christopher Lee, Peter Cushing, Telly Savalas, Silvia Tortosa, Alberto de Mendoza, Helga Line

The Satanic Rites of Dracula (aka **Count Dracula and His Vampire Bride**) (1973) Hammer Films

Directed by Alan Gibson; Screenplay: Don Houghton; Photographer: Brian Probyn; Art Director: Lionel Couch; Editor: Christopher Barnes; Produced by Roy Skeggs

Stars: Christopher Lee, Peter Cushing, William Franklyn, Michael Coles, Joanna Lumley, Freddie Jones

The Wicker Man (1973) A Peter Snell-British Lion Production

Directed by Robin Hardy; Screenplay: Anthony Shaffer; Produced by Peter Snell; Production Designer: Harry Waxman; Editor: Eric Boyd; Music: Paul Giovanni; Assistant Director: Seamus Flannery

Stars: Edward Woodward, Christopher Lee, Britt Ekland, Diane Cilento, Ingrid Pitt, Lindsay Kemp, Russel Waters

The Man with the Golden Gun (1974) United Artists

Directed by Guy Hamilton; Produced by Albert R. Broccoli and Harry Saltzman; Screenplay: Richard Maibaun and Tom Mankiewicz; Based on *The Man with the Golden Gun* by Ian Fleming; Music: John Barry; Photographers: Ted Moore and Oswald Morris; Editors: Raymond Poulton and John Shirley

Stars: Roger Moore, Christopher Lee, Britt Ekland, Maud Adams, Herve Villechaize, Richard Loo, Clifton James

To the Devil a Daughter (1976) Hammer films/Terra Filmkunst

Directed by Peter Sykes; Screenplay: Chris Wicking; Based on the novel by Douglas Wheatley; Photographer: David Watkin; Art Director: Don Picton; Special Effects: Les Bowie; Editor: John Trumper; Produced by Roy Skeggs

Stars: Richard Widmark, Christopher Lee, Honor Blackman, Denholm Elliott, Michael Goodliffe, Nastassja Kinski

Sherlock Holmes and the Leading Lady (1991) Harmony Gold Finance Luxembourg S.A.

Directed by Peter Sasdy; Produced by Harry Alan Towers; Screenplay: Bob Shayne; Music by Detto Mariano

Stars: Christopher Lee, Patrick Macnee, Morgan Fairchild, Tom Lahm, John Bennett

Sherlock Holmes and the Incident at Victoria Falls (1991) Harmony Gold Finance Luxembourg S.A.

Directed by Bill Covcorm; Screenplay: Bob Shayne; Music by Eric Allaman; Produced by Harry Alan Towers

Stars: Christopher Lee, Patrick Macnee, Joss Ackland, Claude Akins, Jenny Seagrove

The Lord of the Rings: The Fellowship of the Ring (2001) WingNut Films, The Saul Zaentz Company

Directed by Peter Jackson; Produced by Barrie M. Osborne, Peter Jackson, Fran Walsh and Tim Sanders; Screenplay: Fran Walsh, Philippa Boyens, Peter Jackson; Based on the novel by J.R.R. Tolkien; Music: Howard Shore; Photographer: Andrew Lesnie; Editor: John Gilbert

Stars: Elijah Wood, Ian McKellen, Liv Tyler, Viggo Mortensen, Sean Astin, Cate Blanchett, John Rhys-Davies, Orlando Bloom, Christopher Lee

The Lord of the Rings: The Two Towers (2002) WingNut Films, The Saul Zaentz Company

Directed by Peter Jackson; Produced by Barrie M. Osborne, Fran Walsh and Peter Jackson; Screenplay: Fran Walsh, Philippa Boyens, Stephen Sinclair and Peter Jackson; Based on the novel by J.R.R. Tolkien; Music: Howard Shore; Editors: Michael Horton and Jabez Olssen

Stars: Elijah Wood, Ian McKellen, Liv Tyler, Viggo Mortensen, Sean Astin, Cate Blanchett, John Thys-Davies, Christopher Lee, Orlando Bloom

Star Wars: Episode II—Attack of the Clones (2002) Twentieth Century–Fox

Directed by George Lucas; Produced by Rick McCallum; Screenplay: George Lucas and Jonathan Hales; Music: John Williams; Photographer: David Tattersall; Editor: Ben Burtt

Stars: Ewan McGregor, Natalie Portman, Hayden Christensen. Ian McDiarmid, Samuel L. Jackson, Christopher Lee, Frank Oz

Star Wars: Episode III—Revenge of the Sith (2005) Twentieth Century–Fox

Directed by George Lucas; Produced by Rick McCallum; Screenplay: George Lucas; Music: John Williams; Photographer: David Tattersall; Editors: Roger Barton and Ben Burtt

Stars: Ewan McGregor, Natalie Portman, Hayden Christensen, Ian McDiarmid, Samuel L. Jackson, Christopher Lee

Commentary on the DVDs of the following films

Dracula, Prince of Darkness The Hammer Collection Anchor Bay, Troy MI 1998

The Devil Rides Out The Hammer Collection Anchor Bay, Troy MI 1998

Flesh and Blood Anchor Bay, Troy MI 1999

Rasputin The Hammer Collection Anchor Bay, Troy MI "World of Hammer: Christopher Lee" 1993

The Wicker Man Anchor Bay, Troy MI 2001

Interviews on the following DVDs

"Christopher Lee: Mr. Holmes, Mr. Wilder" *The Private Life of Sherlock Holmes* King Lorber Twentieth Century–Fox, New York, New York 2014

"Hammer Films" Fanex Files Longthrow Multimedia and Midnight Marquee Productions Narboth, Pennsylvania 2009

"An Actor's Notebook" *The Hound of the Baskervilles* MGM DVD 2002

The Man with the Golden Gun MGM distributed by Twentieth Century–Fox, Beverly Hills, California 2012

Bibliography

Barnes, Alan. *Sherlock Holmes on Screen: The Complete Film and TV History*. London: Reynolds and Hearn, 2002.

Beker, J. Christiaan. *Paul the Apostle: The Triumph of God in Life and Thought*. Philadelphia: Fortress Press, 1980.

Campbell, Joseph. *The Hero with a Thousand Faces*. Princeton (N.J.): Princeton University Press, 1972.

_____. *The Masks of God: Creative Mythology*. New York: Viking Press, 1968.

_____. *The Masks of God: Occidental Mythology*. New York: Viking Press, 1964.

_____. *The Masks of God: Oriental Mythology*. New York: Viking Press, 1962.

_____. *The Masks of God: Primitive Mythology*. New York: Viking Press, 1969.

Chibnall, Steve, and Julian Petley. *British Horror Cinema*. London and New York: Routledge, 2002.

Cotter, Robert Michael "Bobb." *Ingrid Pitt, Queen of Horror: The Complete Career*. Jefferson, NC: McFarland, 2010.

Dunn, James Douglas Grant. *The Theology of the Paul the Apostle*. Grand Rapids, MI: William B. Eerdmans, 1998.

Hardy, Phil. Ed. *The Overlook Film Encyclopedia: Horror*. Woodstock, NY: Overlook Press, 1993.

Hardy, Robin, and Anthony Shaffer. *The Wicker Man*. New York: Crown Publishers, 1978.

Hearn Marcus. *The Art of Hammer*. London: Titan Books, 2010.

_____. *The Hammer Vault*. London: Titan Books, 2010.

_____, and Alan Barnes. *The Hammer Story: The Authorised History of Hammer Films*. London: Titan Books, 2007.

Hunter, Jack, ed. *House of Horror: The Complete Hammer Films Story*, 3rd revised and expanded edition. London: Creation Books, 2000.

Hutchings, Peter. *Dracula*. London: I.B. Tauris, 2003.

_____. *Terence Fisher*. Manchester, U.K.: Manchester University Press, 2001.

Lee, Christopher. *Lord of Misrule: The Autobiography of Christopher Lee*. London: Orion Books, 2003.

Leggett, Paul. *Terence Fisher: Horror, Myth and Religion*. Jefferson, NC: McFarland, 2002.

Lewis, C.S. ed., *Essays Presented to Charles Williams*. Grand Rapids, MI: Eerdmans, 1966.

_____. "Myth Becomes Fact." In *God in the Dock*: Essays *on Theology and Ethics*. Grand Rapids, MI: Eerdmans, 1970.

Maxford, Howard. *Hammer, House of Horror: Behind the Screams*. Woodstock, NY: Overlook Press, 1996.

Meikle, Denis. *A History of Horrors: The Rise and Fall of the House of Hammer*. Lanham, Md.: Scarecrow, 2009.

Pirie, David. *A New Heritage of Horror: The English Gothic Cinema*. London: I.B. Tauris, 2008.

Rigby, Jonathan. *English Gothic: A Century of Horror Cinema*. London: Reynolds and Hearn, 2000.

Rose, James. *Beyond Hammer: British Horror Cinema Since 1970*. Leighton Buzard: Auteur, 2009.

Smith, Gary. *Uneasy Dreams: The Golden Age of British Horror Films 1956–1976*. Jefferson, NC: McFarland, 2000.

Tolkien, J.R.R. *Letters*. Boston: Houghton Mifflin Company, 1981.

_____. "On Fairy Stories" in Lewis, C.S. *Essays Presented to Charles Williams*. Grand Rapids, MI: Eerdmans, 1966.

Index

Numbers in **bold italics** indicate pages with illustrations